CU00704799

THE POWER OF ACCEPTANCE

ONE YEAR OF MINDFULNESS AND MEDITATION

MOLLIE PLAYER

Copyright (C) 2021 Mollie Player

Layout design and Copyright (C) 2021 by Next Chapter

Published 2021 by Next Chapter

Back cover texture by David M. Schrader, used under license from Shutterstock.com

All rights reserved. No part of this book may be reproduced or transmitted in any form or by any means, electronic or mechanical, including photocopying, recording, or by any information storage and retrieval system, without the author's permission.

CONTENTS

Also by Mollie Player   v

January   1
February   11
March   18
April   28
May   43
June   50
July   65
August   81
September   91
December   93
June (the following year)   114
Serenity Prayer, Revised   131
Affirmations   132
Special Section   134

Dear Reader   143
You might also like   145
Also by Mollie Player   147
About the Author   149

ALSO BY MOLLIE PLAYER

Fights You'll Have After Having a Baby: A Self-Help Story

My Byron Katie Detox: One Year of Questioning My Unhelpful Thoughts

You're Getting Closer: One Year of Finding God and a Few Good Friends

The Naked House: Five Principles for a More Peaceful Home

What I Learned from Jane

Unicorn

Being Good

For free ebooks and online serials by Mollie Player, visit mollieplayer.com.

This book is only mostly true.

For Leta. Love you.

JANUARY
CLICK!

I WISH I could remember the exact phrase that got it into me, that finally made it go *click!* But maybe there wasn't one; maybe it was the book as a whole that implanted it, in some otherworldly, sibylline way. Whatever the case, soon afterward came the more important moment, the one I remember to this day.

It was the summer of 2013. I was sitting in our family room reading Eckhart Tolle's *The Power of Now* as the baby played next to me on a big green comforter on the floor. As he mouthed one unsuspecting rattle after another and pressed buttons that rewarded him with nonsense, I finished the book for the third time. And though I still don't know the exact point at which it happened, by the time I set the book down, something inside me had changed. I put a hand on Xavier's fresh little face and he turned to me, looking disoriented. I smiled and he held my gaze and smiled back, then held out his stubby arms. I pulled him into my lap and his head bobbed toward my breast and as I nursed him I considered what I'd just read.

Though I had been raised immersed (some may say half-drowned) in religion, the several years leading up to Xavier's conception had been focused elsewhere—mostly on my new partner, David, and my growing freelance writing business. Spirituality was still there—part of me, part of my definition of myself—but it wasn't very close to the surface.

Then, a year before the baby was born, I discovered *Conversations with God* by Neale Donald Walsch, and with it a strange brand of spirituality called New Thought. By the time I picked up *The Power of Now* for the third time, a year and a half had passed, and Xavier was about six months old. I had explored and applied my new beliefs in depth, and now it was time to take the next step. Long days of motherhood begged for community and friendship, as well as increased inner strength. And so, to my still-unfamiliar routine of play dates, car naps and Gymboree, I added going to church.

Another book of mine discusses my attempt to fulfill a two-pronged goal to increase both earthly and divine connection. Meditation was a logical part of the plan, but there was a problem: until that day on the floor with Tolle and baby, I had never truly tried it. Once, while I was still a Christian, I attended one Buddhist meditation session in a home that had been revamped into a temple, but this hardly counted; it was cultural voyeurism, not a sincere effort. It was a minor act of rebellion, of open-mindedness, a pushing of the envelope, the kind of thing a good girl like myself found exciting.

Except one thing: It wasn't exciting—not at all. Not the least little bit. In that room decorated all in red—red velvet pillows, red calligraphy wall hangings, red-patterned plush carpet—I could hardly breathe for the effort it took to sit still. And when I tried to focus on my breath, as the unsmiling leader suggested, I nearly hyper-ventilated.

And that was just the first five minutes.

Soon, I gave up, and instead watched the clock and the handful of people sitting with me. *How do they do it?* I wondered as my back started aching and my legs fell asleep. *More to the point,* why *do they?*

I shifted out of the kneeling position and moved against the back wall. I considered leaving, but didn't.

Slowly, slowly, time dripped from the clock, and the final instruction—to open our eyes—came as a relief. I got out of there as fast as possible, shoes in hand, and fidgeted my way to the car.

Which is why it was strange that after finishing *The Power of Now* that day twelve years later, I decided to try it again.

Like I said: something had clicked.

Sitting on the green blanket, Xavier still in my arms, I flipped back through the pages of the book I hadn't wanted to read again, then hadn't wanted to finish. I looked for a passage I'd underlined about Tolle's unique meditation technique, namely, sensing the energy of the body, then reread it several times.

You know what? I thought, *This doesn't sound so bad. I don't even have to stop thinking. What if it really can help me connect with the Divine inside myself?*

What if it actually works?

I closed my eyes. I tried to sense my body, as Tolle instructed—to feel the subtle energy moving in and through me. It didn't take long before I realized that it was working: I could feel it. It was there. This was real.

I felt the tingling of my hands. I felt the pulsing of my arms and legs. Though I knew it was probably just a body being a body, noticing it in this way was calming. Suddenly, it hit me: I was meditating. And it wasn't even that hard.

That evening I took a long walk with the baby and tried the technique again. This time, I didn't think of it as meditation—I wasn't sitting, after all—but the feeling I had was the same. I was relaxed, but it was more than that: I was present. I was in a now-place in my mind, rather than in the future or the past. There was a subtle joy and a feeling of love that accompanied this presence, too, which I considered to be some sort of connection with the Divine. And so, the following day I decided to take the next step: I looked up meditation classes in my area.

Not long after that, I was hooked.

Before I knew it, Xavier was one year old and I had spent the past six sleep-deprived months honing this newly-discovered skill. The following year, as I wrote *You're Getting Closer*, I expanded my spiritual practices considerably, with success following disappointment following success.

A year passed. Xavier was now two years old, and as I reflected on that milestone in his life I thought about my own progress, too.

And one of the things I thought about most was my failure.

———

Last November, sometime in the middle of the month, I had the best two weeks of my year. After a couple of particularly enjoyable incidents—one being a trip to see my family—a warm, delicious feeling got into me and stuck, and every day—nearly every moment, even—I felt the presence of God.

I felt it when I read. I felt it when I played with my child. It was there all the time, a bit below the surface of my thoughts. Even when difficulties arose, the state of mind remained; I was able to stay an arm's length from my problems. At one point during this time, for example, a friend got upset at me for not cleaning up the mess my kids had made at her house. Though our hour-long conversation about it was tense and uncomfortable, delving into past slights and wrongs, I got though it without anger. A few days later, on my most enjoyable birthday in recent memory, I told my husband I felt deeply at peace.

Then one day, a week or so later, that special feeling went away. I still don't know why it happened. Maybe I'd become complacent, or maybe I wasn't mediating as much, or maybe it was a new bout of depression coming on. Whatever the cause, it was a great disappointment—one that represented a much larger problem.

This wasn't the only time a spiritual high was followed by a major low that year—or the year before, for that matter. And so one day toward the end of that year, I attempted to figure all this out.

What am I doing wrong? I asked God over and over. *More importantly, what was I doing right before that I am not doing now?*

And I didn't just pray. Every day for a month straight, I tried every trick I knew to get the feeling back. Of course, meditation was the first on my list, as it had been for the past year and a half. I upped my weekly goals from one class to three, enlisting my husband's support. He took the baby swimming while I went to church or temple, seeking that spiritual high. The hour-long sessions were helpful, but they didn't get me out of my rut. Neither did my mantras or my visualizations—or my walks, which often incorporated both.

I still felt pretty crappy.

And so, for a while, I stopped trying. I gave up. I was tired of all the effort, the fruitless striving. I needed a break, but what I didn't realize was that more than four months would pass before I even attempted another sitting meditation.

The time off wasn't a total loss. During it, I thought about what I needed that I didn't have—the missing link, so to speak. Intuitively I knew that there was some method I could use anytime, no matter how I felt, that would immediately get me in touch with the Divine. After all, all of the New Thought mentors out there say that spiritual connectedness is our natural state. So why, after several years of striving and seeking, was I still feeling it so infrequently?

Truly, I was missing something.

With this goal in mind, I resumed my current spiritual practices as well as my search for more effective ones. I read more books, discovered more techniques—prayers and ideas I hadn't yet tried. I counteracted negative thoughts with positive ones, as the collective entity known as Abraham recommends. I re-read *You're Getting Closer* and became inspired to again surrender each moment to divine guidance. But while these practices and many like them brought some encouragement, some peace, I never got back to where I was.

I am still not back. Currently, I'm swimming upstream, as Abraham says, very much against the current of the spirit. My thoughts are often negative. My mood is often recalcitrant. Most of the time, I want to be somewhere else. I'm easily annoyed, and easily insulted, and often downright neurotic.

In other words: I'm not feeling very spiritual.

It is the beginning of January, however, and if there's anything I love, it's a fresh start. Sure, it's only a date on the calendar—but it may be just the thing I need.

It's time for a New Year's resolution.

———

Although it was long before the beginning of the year that I decided to make a spiritually minded resolution, until a few days ago I knew only the criteria. The goal, I realized, would have to be doable, something I could stick to all year. It would have to allow for imperfection, and maybe lots of it, and be simple and clearly stated. When one pen, two pieces of paper, my favorite chair and thirty free minutes collided in my world, I sat down to consider my options.

Should I do a sitting meditation every day, and if so, how long should it last? Would five minutes be enough to make it worth the effort, or should I do at least fifteen?

Should I resume my goal to hold myself in continuous meditation all day long? And if so, how would I do it? Would I say mantras, visualize my God-self, listen for action-by-action guidance? Or should I try something else entirely?

Finally, I made the decision. My twofold resolution this year isn't as bold as my last—and not nearly as frightening, either. I will do sitting meditation for at least five minutes every day, and I'll remain in the state of meditation as much a possible after that.

Five minutes is doable every day, I realized as the idea came—even for a busy mom like me. It's simple and easy to track, and if I'm able to stick with it, the benefits could be enormous. But what really convinced me to choose this goal was that, compared with other options, it's relatively low-pressure.

––––––

Recently, I was reflecting on some of the spiritual books I love that draw so many other people in, too, and with such devotion. *Why do I like Eckhart Tolle so much?* I asked myself. *And Neale Donald Walsch, and Esther Hicks?*

Is it because they're so quotable, so poetic? Somehow, I don't think that's it. Is it because they claim to hear directly from a divine Source? Maybe, but Tolle doesn't channel his books.

The number one reason we love them so much, I believe, is this: they are extreme. They don't merely describe a nice spiritual practice, or summarize a few lofty ideas. They aren't conservative. They don't hold back. Instead, they insist we can all be great. We can all get enlightened. And maybe even healthy and wealthy, too. Barring these goals, we can at least experience something we've been seeking a long time: our next major spiritual high.

And we believe them. We read them, then read them again, then try to practice what they preach. Our efforts pay off: we get a glimpse of the bliss they promise. Then we read the next book and wait for more.

Many of us—most of us—are still waiting.

Of course, our frequent failed attempts at inner peace are not the fault of these wonderful authors. Bliss, enlightenment, our next spiritual high—these are, as they say, truly possible for us all. The problem is this: obsessing about where we're headed doesn't help the car drive faster; if anything, it tends to slow it down.

Which is why five minutes of meditation feels right to me this year. It isn't an overly optimistic goal. It isn't going to cause me to expect fast miracles, or spiritual ascendance overnight.

If anything, it'll remind me to stay humble.

And although the second part of my resolution is much like that in *You're Getting Closer*, namely, remaining in continuous communication with the Divine, there's one important difference here. That difference comes in the middle part of the sentence: "as much as possible."

As much as possible. As much as I can.

In a way, the qualifier is an escape clause—a way out of my resolution, should I need one. But I know me, and perfection can't be my goal. If it is, I'll just give up. And that seems pretty counter-productive, doesn't it?

When I'm an old woman, with cropped curly hair, and eight pink sweaters and one pair of brown shoes, I'm going to be good at being spiritual. I'll have one of those blissed-out smiles for everyone, and upbeat catch phrases like "You do you, Martha!" I'll be wise, and silly, and sane, too, damn it. Damn it, damn it, damn it: I will. Until then, though, I'll just be consistent. I'll just do the work that will eventually get me to that point. Every day, for five minutes, I'll seek a peaceful mental place. And when I find it, I'll try to stay a while.

As it turns out, I'm not Eckhart Tolle—or Esther Hicks, for that matter. I'm just a regular person, muddling my way through, hoping for a few answers to the usual questions, such as those I'm asking this year:

- Will I be able to keep my resolution this year to meditate for five minutes a day?
- Will I find it hard to do so, or will it be fairly easy?
- Will I get rid of any part of my neurotic tendencies? Or will they mostly remain?
- Maybe most important, will I find the missing link I'm looking for—a continuous meditation method that works every time?

I have no idea whether or not the perfect spiritual practice is out there, or whether there's some other, more important lesson in store. But isn't the process of discovery a major part of the fun?

Seeking is what makes the finding interesting.

FEBRUARY
SOMETIMES, THE MAJORITY IS RIGHT

LAST MONTH I proved myself right—sort of. I proved I've been doing something wrong for some time, and that what I'm doing now is better.

Today is February 26th, and every day for the two months since I last wrote, I've sat and meditated for five minutes. The takeaway: Whereas in the past I was convinced that this small goal would be difficult (what about the baby? And my morning exhaustion? What about when I'm just in a bad mood?), I now firmly believe otherwise.

So far, these shorter but more frequent sessions have been not only easier than expected, but more effective as well. They're enjoyable, and inspiring, and well worth the effort. It's like all those cheerful churchgoers say: a little bit of quiet time each day is the best thing for growth.

I guess sometimes the majority is right.

Here, a description of my practice so far.

Though any location is a good enough location for meditation, my usual routine takes place on my family room floor. As Xavier explores the various temptations I've spread out for him, I lean against a cushion and close my eyes. As I lay my hands on my legs, then turn up both palms, my attention falls on the tingling and warmth I find there. I choose a mantra that seems to hit the right note, then repeat it silently over and over. Notably, I do not try to stop thinking; instead, I carefully direct my thoughts. If my mantra has to do with the energy in my body, I imagine it coursing through me, cell by cell. If my mantra has to do with the kind of person I want to be, I enjoy visualizing every detail. Nothing new or original here, but there is something that's surprised me about my new, more consistent routine, namely: it usually feels good—even when I don't.

Previously I believed, albeit subconsciously, that if I wasn't in the right mood, meditation wouldn't work. I dreaded sitting for any length of time feeling uninspired and frustrated—even for five minutes. Even for one. But this morning, I woke up overtired and annoyed, yet when I closed my eyes, I felt the same as I always do. There was a buzz of sorts, a feeling of loving observation. It felt like the whole world was just me, my hands and God.

Best of all: as I sat, some of the tension that had been hiding under my skin seemed to break into pieces. The anger and annoyance, particularly around my eyes and mouth, disseminated, then escaped out my pores. This evening, when David came home from work and I remembered our argument from last night, both of us noticed the lighter mood.

It was an argument, my new face said. *Really not a big deal.*

Five minutes of meditation a day isn't going to solve all my problems, smooth out every lump, bump and imperfection. But

I'm looking forward to seeing the big change that the small changes will make—all the fine lines that replace the deep ones.

———

One Sunday morning at my Unitarian Universalist church, a nine-year-old girl sat on the floor facing her chair. As she played with ribbons, eventually constructing a bracelet, I sat directly facing her, eyes closed and palms raised. Together, we remained seated for the whole length of the service, even when asked to stand. She was my fellow holdout, in unspoken cahoots—an ally I didn't know by name.

Often, I feel self-conscious when I meditate in public, and church is no exception. That day, though, I had a semi-valid excuse for my inhibition: the girl was sneaking glances at me as often as I did her. My mind wandered: *Did she know I was meditating? Did she think it strange?*

Nine is the age of curiosity. But then, so is thirty-six. Her questioning glances caused me to question myself: What exactly was I doing, anyway?

What is this thing we call meditation?

When the service was over, and we stood to leave, I smiled at the girl and waved goodbye. She waved back, then ducked her head, turning to her mom. As I watched her file out, it came.

"Meditation is when you sit very still, and maybe close your eyes, and feel the feeling of feeling good."

It's not the definition you usually hear—but as I soon realized, none of them are.

———

After my first and solo attempt at meditation, I decided to start taking classes. I did a bit of research and was surprised to encounter a large number of interesting options.

I'm definitely going to find what I'm looking for, I thought as I bookmarked every group in my area. I was right—but it took some time.

One of the first group meditations I attended was held at a house-turned-bookstore one suburb over. When I got there, I wondered if I was in the right place: no teacher, no one tending the store. I looked for a bell but found nothing.

Ten minutes later, a troop of stylish hippies walked in: two young women, a young man, and a middle-aged man, clearly the leader. They wore the kind of clothes that are made to look bohemian but aren't: for the men, pre-faded jeans and expertly crafted leather sandals, and for the women, skintight Lycra workout clothes paired with flower-patterned accessories.

Immediately, I felt out of place: the newcomer clad in tennis shoes and my husband's cast off T-shirt. I didn't even have a yoga mat.

"Welcome," said the leader, who I immediately thought of as the Guru, as the group noticed me perusing the books. "I apologize for the wait. We just got back from a hike." His voice was airy, breathless, and deliberate, like an author being interviewed on NPR.

As the other attendees avoided my tentative greeting glances, the Guru fumbled around looking for his keys. He led us to one of the doors lining the long hallway, then unlocked it and entered the room.

"Come in," he said as he took his place behind a large desk. "Choose a space you like and get comfortable."

The first to follow, I chose a fold-up chair near the wall, but it was the wrong thing to do. One by one, the others unrolled their mats and assumed the classic yoga pose, crossing their legs and keeping their back straight.

I slumped in my chair a bit further.

After a brief, generic introduction, the session officially began. The Guru began guiding us through various sensual scenarios, his breathy voice sucking in more air than ever.

"Think about water, how it sounds, how it feels, how it winds its way through the world with such ease. For the next few minutes, you are that water. Imagine it. Visualize it. Feel it. Let it be."

And I did. I closed my eyes and thought about water and the other elements he described, but instead of feeling Zen, I felt bored. I wished that I had just tuned the whole thing out, and stuck with my own tried-and-true technique.

When the hour was over, the Guru asked us to describe our experiences. One of the women volunteered to go first.

"There was an inner movement," she said, in a voice nearly as breathy as the Guru's. "It went in a pattern, like a figure eight. I felt myself moving with it, over and over." She swayed her hands appropriately in the air.

I raised my eyebrows with the surprise of the uninitiated, then looked to the Guru for his reaction. His approving smile made me want to roll my eyes, but instead I just averted them quickly.

The young man went next, discussing a "clown-like angelic presence" and the second woman said she "entered the void." Then it was my turn to speak.

"It felt ... good," I said lamely, shifting in my chair. "I felt ... something. It was nice."

The Guru hesitated, then nodded slowly, his dark brow furrowed a bit. To cover the silence and attempt to salvage the moment, I tacked on hastily, "I've mediated a lot before, I just haven't taken a class."

Immediately, I regretted the out-of-context comment. *Why can't I ever be cool?*

"I see." The Guru smiled. "Well, this class is for advanced mediators, people who have already learned the technique. We have other classes for beginners. I suggest that next time you come to one of those."

"Oh, okay," I said, but what I thought was, *Elitist meditation? Really too bad that's a thing.*

The class ended, and the students gathered at the teacher's desk to ask questions and (presumably) plan their next hike. He interrupted one of them to hand me something.

The Guru, it turned out, had a business card.

"Want to reduce your stress?" I read as I walked to my car. "The art of meditation is the art of relaxation. First class free."

I drove home that night knowing I would never return—no matter how many angels and figure eights I learned to sense. Meditation, I realized then, can't be bought or sold, and no one teacher or technique is the best. It's personal, and varied, and incredibly complex: a feeling, a knowing, ineffable.

Over the year that followed, I met a lot of meditators, and many of them disagreed with this perspective. The practice they loved most had worked well for them. Why wouldn't it do the same for others?

It's a good question—one I asked many times in the years to come, and still ask on occasion. It would be so much simpler if we all just did the same thing. Then I remember: what fun would that be?

The fun is in the discovery.

MARCH

BEING IN THE MOMENT SUCKS (OR DO I JUST SUCK AT IT?)

IF I NEVER AGAIN HEAR THE phrase "in the moment," I won't miss it a bit. Like many other spirituality clichés ("letting go," "surrendering" and "being at peace with what is," to name a few), it's far too unspecific for my taste. What does "in the moment" even mean, anyway? Feeling happy about whatever I'm experiencing right now? What if I'm just ... not?

And yes, the fact remains that being in the moment is one of the things I most need to learn. If I'm going to do this continuous meditation thing, I need to drastically lessen my preoccupation with the future and the past—to let go, to surrender, and yes, to be at peace with what is.

Esther Hicks and Abraham call present moment awareness "the vortex," and I really like this metaphor. When you're in the vortex, everything's heightened—your power, your energy, your abilities. It's not unlike what happens when you capture the invincibility star in a Super Mario Brothers video game. The music changes, and speeds up. You start glowing and changing color. Most important, every enemy that dares cross your path dies at the merest blow.

That's the vortex and that's the state of meditation. Unfortunately, it's one that often eludes me. Apparently it's one thing to get up in the morning and meditate for a few minutes quietly, alone, and quite another to hold onto that feeling when distracted. So far this year, I've rarely done so.

There are reasons for this, of course; there are always reasons for these things. I've been sick a lot. And feeling a bit lonely, since my husband has been working overtime. Oh, and lest I forget to mention, I'm currently pregnant: well into my second trimester, and exhausted. But this is life, after all, just life; and along with the good, there's the rest.

And really, there is a lot of good. Right now, I'm lounging in a comfy beach chair wearing yoga pants (my favorite pair of the twelve I own). I'm sipping freshly brewed coffee and looking on as Xavier plays in a sandbox the size of two volleyball courts. Surrounded by some of his favorite things—trucks, wagons and slides—he's content, which makes my job pretty easy. When the toddler is happy, I should be, too—and yet, currently I'm not.

In fact, I'm kinda depressed.

Even with an amazing child, and a wonderful husband, and spiritual awareness and an optimistic love-based understanding of the Divine. Even with consistent meditation, and all material things I really need.

Even with, even with, even with.

And so, the time has come for a change, and the change I'm making is a plan—clearly stated, and with instructions.

In *You're Getting Closer* I listed all of the techniques I've used in the past to get into my good-feeling spiritual place. And even though my results with them have been mixed, they're still the best options that I have. They are:

- Asking my higher self for moment-by-moment guidance (where should I go right now? What should I do?);
- Replacing negative thoughts with positive ones continually;
- Saying mantras and affirmations;
- Doing visualizations;
- Mentally noting everything I'm grateful for;
- Bringing my attention back to my "inner body"—the spirit energy that emanates from me— throughout the day;
- Doing a sitting meditation;
- Journaling;
- Listening to music while focusing on love energy;
- Reading spiritual books;
- Smiling, even when I don't feel like it;
- Doing nice things for others while sending them love energy; and
- Continually reminding myself of the presence of the Divine.

The first part of my plan is this: Each morning after meditation, I will choose one of these techniques to try throughout the day. No tracking, no obsessing, perfection not required—I will just do the best I can. The second part: I'll do the research. I'll read a ton of books on spirituality and meditation, looking for new in-the-vortex techniques to add to my list.

Maybe then the invincibility star will be mine.

Incidentally, it's not just my frustration with my New Year's goals that inspired this plan. A few weeks ago, I read a book called *10 Percent Happier: How I Tamed the Voice in My Head, Reduced Stress Without Losing My Edge, and Found Self-Help That Actually Works—A True Story* by agnostic news anchor Dan Harris. In it, he relates in detail his discovery of meditation, explaining how it helped him become a better, happier individual. His method: the classic breath-focused awareness. He listens to his breath and attempts to clear his mind, bringing his attention back to his breath when it wanders. One of the main takeaways is that learning meditation is a lot like learning a sport: every time you practice, you get better. Enjoying it—feeling good, doing it right—is not the goal. Just doing it regularly is. Sitting in the chair, trying again—"That's the whole game," he says.

This assertion, which I've heard before, made me wonder: Is he right? If meditation isn't a feeling, what is it? Maybe I don't know as much about it as I think I do.

Maybe I am doing it all wrong.

I don't watch my breath. I've tried it and I hated it. It just caused me to hyperventilate. And I certainly don't try not to think, as others do. Having a focal point, often a mantra, helps me stay on task.

That said, maybe there's something to these techniques that is ultimately superior to my own. That early meditation class I went to during which I felt so inferior, so unpracticed—maybe there was good reason for that. Maybe everyone knows something I don't yet know. Either way, I need to find out; I need to get reading.

I will of course let you know what I learn.

———

MEDITATION INTERVIEW #1: The Buddhist

While editing this manuscript, I sensed something was missing —but I couldn't quite figure out what. Then, it hit me: I'm not that good at meditation. What this book needs is a nice big dose of expertise.

I hope you enjoy the seven interviews (and one bonus interview) with long-time meditators interspersed throughout these pages; I sure did.

First up: Art and meditation teacher Carrie Coe Phillips. Carrie is a careful, conscientious person. When I first met her, I was immediately attracted to her kindness, which shows clearly in her face. Then I got to know her and realized she's not just a nice person—she's quite wise, too.

Do you have inner peace?

A lot of the time, I do. It's not all of the time. I deal with fear, health concerns. And I have backup for that–when I put it to use.

When I first started meditating, I felt ecstatically good. When you're young and healthy, you feel totally in your life and loving it. These days I can say that the journey is not about happiness. It's about self-discovery, about opening up, and about making yourself available to others.

Is it possible for anyone to find inner peace?

Yes, it is. Through meditation. I believe they must meditate.

All of us need brief interludes of non-conceptual experience. If someone wants a genuine spiritual path then I would include shamatha practice as well. (Not all meditations perform the same service. The one I'm speaking of is Calm Abiding or resting the mind, shamatha in Sanskrit. This is where the mindfulness movement found its source.)

Everyone is so absorbed in overwhelming struggles, getting just a slight view of "no-self" is helpful. Even someone with the least bit of curiosity can easily experience a shift in how they view what's going on.

What do you mean by "no-self"?

The "no-self" that I speak of is from a basic tenet of Buddhism that proposes the lack of inherent existence in all phenomenon. Briefly, all things exist relatively. Everything that exists does so in reaction and relation to something else. There is how things appear and how things truly are from the perspective of enlightened mind. When we loosen our grip on a solid-self through meditation, and also through a combination of contemplation on the study of and or listening to the teachings of qualified teachers, then in my experience the path to "freedom" reveals itself in a myriad of ways.

Some forms of spirituality are more rule-based than others. In my limited experience with Buddhism, it seems that it is somewhere in-between the extremes: not particularly dogmatic,

but at the same time, often prescriptive. What do you think?

It can be dogmatic. It doesn't have to be.

Has there ever been a time in your life when you truly questioned everything that you believe? How did you circle back to where you are now? Tell me the story.

Every so often I wonder why there have to be so many images in Buddhism. Coming from a background in which there's a restriction against statues and images, it bothers me a bit.

I get different explanations for why they're there. One is that historically the statues weren't a part of it, and they were only added later after the Silk Road opened up (due to the influence of Greek imagery), and therefore they aren't a needed part of the practice. Another is that the images are representations of enlightened energy, an enlightened mind. There is a myriad of methods for people at different stages of practice; some work for some people but not others.

What if you're wrong about your faith? What if after death you find out that Buddhism is just partly true, or not true?

The Tibetan Buddhist teachings on both the death process and the afterdeath process are unlike any other teachings. There are very careful instructions on what to do. I have complete faith in these Tibetan teachings.

You know, when you meditate with some consistency, your mind will want to wake you up to the truth. Then, when you look around, when you listen to or read what's been written by other meditators, and your truth matches the other person's truth ... now you are on to something. You have insight.

What do you mean by insight? What kind of insight?

By insight I mean a momentary flash of wisdom. You might not even recall it but it changes you on a deep level. Buddhists also call it clarity.

Do you have clarity? How much do you have, would you say?

Sure, I have some. There's no way of telling how much. I can say that the more I meditate the more the chances are that I will.

Do you mean do I have flashes of insight? Sometimes. It's not something you go looking for; you can't direct it. And as I said before, the difference between ordinary insight (which will also increase with meditation) and true spiritual insight is that you will probably not remember true spiritual insight after it happens.

What would you say to someone who is struggling with depression?

I'm not a stranger to depression, and I have two close family members that have struggled with depression most of their lives. Both have a daily meditation practice. My best advice is, don't use your meditation for your depression. Use your depression for your meditation.

Interesting. What do you mean by that, exactly?

I mean that if you're looking to meditation for happiness, and you hit a bump in the road—then what do you do? Do you give up? Do you find something to blame? Look at depression as something to meditate with rather than looking at meditation as something to cure depression.

Meditate on depression means to be with it, not to contemplate it while meditating. You can add a brief contemplative practice before or after your session of meditation if you like.

What else? Any other thoughts on depression?

The advice that I take from Pema Chodron is to lean in to the sharp points. If you're feeling this wretchedness anyway, what have you got to lose by opening up to it and saying, "Okay, here I am, give me your worst"? You feel whatever you're feeling and don't reject it. If you can do that even for five seconds, the next time it may be seven seconds. And you're on your way.

Life is all about patterns. These patterns, whether negative or positive, are reinforced when you're distracted. But when you watch the patterns, meditate, your mind slows down and they start to weaken. You come back to the present moment—often some sensation in your body—and watch that. Some say to feel your inner body ("What's my toe doing right now?") and others follow their breath, but if you have a strong sensation happening anywhere in your body, you go there. If it's distracting enough that you aren't able to focus on the breath, go there. This includes heart-based feelings like sadness.

Don't go to the depression with concepts. Go to it without labeling it. Just notice the primary feeling—where it is in your body, how it feels, Just notice and send gentleness. At this point, it may be uncomfortable but it's no longer fear-producing. And it's the fear of that pain that makes it seem unbearable, not the pain itself.

Pema's first teacher—and author, artist, poet and great

meditation master–Chögyam Trungpa Rinpoche said: "Put the fearful mind in the cradle of loving kindness." Love yourself, however you find yourself. Identify yourself as part of all the other living beings that you're practicing love for, too.

In short: Make friends with your depression.

APRIL

THE PERFECTION OF A NAP AND A WALK

GREAT NEWS THIS MONTH: I'm meditating. Continuously. (Finally.)

I'm finally in the state of meditation.

It didn't happen as a result of The List, however. Or my five-minute habit, or the books. Though I've enjoyed these experiences with some frequency, they weren't enough to turn this boat around.

My thoughts were still largely negative.

Does Abraham realize how hard this is for me? I wondered in frustration. *This whole getting in the vortex, continuous meditation thing? Does Seth or Archangel Michael know what it's like to have a less than carefree natural disposition?*

When you're already heading downstream, of course, it feels natural and easy to continue. But when you're trying to turn the rudder, it's a pain.

And then—miracle of miracles!—it happened. I finally managed to change directions. All it took was a really big push.

That push happened on a swing.

Now, admittedly, a lengthy setup was involved. It started with a three-hour nap with Xavier. (This is something I'd been needing for a while.) Then together we took a beautiful evening walk, during which I listed, out loud, what I was grateful for that day.

I was grateful for the flowers, now in full bloomingest bloom; for the trees, recently reclothed in green. I was grateful for the ducks that greeted us eagerly as ever. And I was grateful when Xavier, content in his stroller till now, uttered his favorite of all words. It was his word for nursing: "boo-boo."

Since we were just then passing our favorite sitting spot—a large porch swing with a view of the lake—his request was easily accommodated. I parked the stroller near the cabin and climbed the stairs, Xavier wrapped in a blanket to keep the wind off his body. With his face buried in my chest, I sat in the swing, then began pushing my feet against the railing in front of it: knees up, push, legs up, swing. Knees up, push, legs up, swing.

Maybe it was the cold that kept Xavi from squirming out of the blankets, or maybe it was the motion of the swing. Whatever the case, for nearly forty-five minutes he was silent and content —and I, too, became calm. As I looked at the lake and the trees and the street far beyond where a steady stream of headlights moved evenly through the dark, I finally felt the feeling of feeling good.

When I got home that night, I continued my gratitude meditation, noting with joy the small blessings. I focused on the feeling, just sat with it, refusing to let myself get distracted. The next day, and the next, when something didn't go my way, I immediately found a way to feel better. I bought a new book. Planned a trip. Breathed deeply. Drank some coffee. I did what I could to get through it.

That was two weeks ago, and I'm happy to report that the feeling has been with me ever since. One day at a time, I found a way to feel good. Then I didn't let the good day go.

In Super Mario Brothers, the clearest progress is made when the player completes another level. Ever after, till the game is over, she holds her new place, re-starting there when she dies.

Maybe it's optimistic, even naive, but it feels like this discovery is a similar kind of achievement.

Spiritually speaking, I may have leveled up.

For fourteen days straight, I've had invincibility, holding onto the star even through challenges. More important, I may have discovered a way to get it back when I lose it: by simply doing more things I enjoy.

If the feeling of feeling good really is the feeling of meditation—what's the difference what the feeling is about? Maybe instead of first meditating, then getting the feeling of it, I can come at it from the opposite side. I can get the good feeling, then turn it into meditation by remembering the divine nature of that joy. I can thank God, or think loving thoughts, and there! That's it. That's the star.

I can do what I can to have a good day—then not let the good day go.

———

The recorded voice, with its relaxing musical accompaniment, was serene yet authoritative. Which may be why. though no one else was in the room with me, I felt compelled to do what it said.

"Sit on folded legs in a kneeling posture, back straight. Then place your right hand on your stomach. Breathe in deeply, then hold your breath there, noticing all sensations that occur. Send love to the area, love, love. Now let the breath out and stand." Instructions like these, highly detailed, somewhat difficult, came one after the other. There was bowing, and hand motioning, and yoga-like calisthenics, and a whole lot of sitting up straight. Soon, my arm was shaking, and my legs fast asleep —but what really bothered me was my back.

I do not have good posture. It's tiring. It's painful. And for some reason it makes it hard for me to breathe. So when after my encounter with the Guru I decided to try a traditional Buddhist meditation at a traditional Buddhist temple (complete with statues), it didn't go so well.

Buddhists, man, I tell ya. They're for real.

Though I never learned exactly what type of meditation this was supposed to be, I knew the point was to transcend my discomfort. The pain would help me access my inner resources, I figured. And I really liked the idea.

In fact, I liked everything about the place: the gold statues, the colorful array of sacred objects, the curtain made of tiny purple beads. I even liked that I was the only one who showed up that evening, and that there wasn't even a live leader, just a really good sound system. It was sort of like having my very own Hal, the artificial intelligence in *2001: A Space Odyssey*. The voice, though disembodied, was wise and fatherly, and in a rare mom moment, I got to be alone.

So I was disappointed that I hated it so much.

I didn't make it through that whole class. When the fourth chakra was fully blessed and explored, Hal mentioned that there were three more to go. *Seven chakras?* I thought. I turned to check the clock once again. It had only been a half hour.

Holy God, I'm only halfway through.

I took a deep breath, then got that feeling that you get during the cobra pose in Bikram yoga, the one where you sort of (or more than sort of) want to cry. But yoga classes are usually filled with pretty, judgy people, often with perfect posture, all of whom would see you leave.

There were no such people here.

I looked away from the clock, then slumped my shoulders, curling them far over my stomach.

Ah, that's better, I thought, stretching out my legs. *Maybe I'll just ignore the instructions and do this my own way.*

Then I thought, *Or maybe not.*

With a quick glance around the room, I stood up and grabbed my shoes. Then I snuck out of the room. When I got outside, I cleared the doors and windows.

Then I put on my shoes.

Hal was still in there, still talking, still bowing, on and on forevermore. He was stuck in that sound system, in that one ornate room.

I, however, was not.

Awesome things happen when you transcend your pain. I get it, I really do. Embracing discomfort isn't only for hair-shirted monks; modern-day seekers benefit, too. In *Eat, Pray, Love,* the super cool Elizabeth Gilbert talks about meditating while mosquitoes feasted on her flesh. And in *Sex, Drugs, and Meditation: How One Woman Changed Her Life, Saved Her Job and Found a Husband,* Mary Lou Stephens endures a tortuous ten days of stillness and silence in a desperate attempt to fix her broken life.

In my car the evening of my great meditation escape, however, I came to a decision that holds to this day: I'm just not a pain kind of person. Pregnancy nausea, exhaustion, parenthood and marriage, plus regular bouts of inimical depression—in spite of the many great blessings in my life, when I need challenges, I have them. They help me grow, they help me remember what's important, but what they don't help me do is meditate.

If enlightenment ever happens to me, it likely won't be during an all-night vigil or a fast. It'll probably happen after a nap and a walk.

———

MEDITATION INTERVIEW #2: The Channel

*Second up: my good friend and mentor **Leta Hamilton**. Summing up this earthy-yet-otherworldly creature called Leta in a paragraph is certainly no easy task. At first glance, she's a suburban mother of four who wears multiple bracelets on both arms and long scarves. Dig just a little deeper, though, and suddenly you're talking to someone else entirely, someone you* *really didn't expect: an accomplished author and a channel for the angels. Either way, you can learn a lot from Leta.*

Tell me what your definition of meditation is—just your own. (Don't cheat.)

Breathing with presence and awareness of breath. Breathing intentionally. Breathing and knowing that you are breathing. Breathing in and out with a mindfulness about the breath. Then, as you move through your day, things come and go and you are present to them. Life becomes a walking meditation.

Describe for me your meditation practice.

I do a sitting meditation of five minutes a day where I am just sitting and breathing. Sometimes it lasts longer, but it's always at least five minutes. Then I go back to my breath at all times of the day. I am praying consistently throughout the day. Not a prayer for something, just prayer. Life as a prayer. Life as a meditation. I pray peace, as my being-ness in the world. I pray in my heart with the mantra God, God, God. I say, "This—this —this is God." I love what is and if I don't love something, I watch myself as the observer and notice that I am not loving it and I love that I am not loving it. I step back and watch myself be in a situation and I love that.

What might you tell a new meditator to help them through the first part of the learning process?

Breathe. Breath is so important. Just listening to yourself breathe in and out, in and out, in and out. That is enough. Five minutes of just breathing. Then, notice your breath throughout the day. Always go back to the breath. Remember to breathe consciously, mindfully and with presence. When you think of it, breathe. At all times of the day, remember to take a deep breath in and a deep breath out. You are breathing, breathing, breathing and suddenly, life becomes the meditation. Meditation and prayer come together in harmony because you are no longer praying as a plea for something to change, you are being the prayer.

How long have you been practicing meditation?

Meditation has been in my life since my second child was six months old and my first was three and a half. That is about eight years. We used to walk William to his preschool and I would go walking with Oliver after drop off. He usually slept in his buggy and I would sit on a bench outside if the weather was decent or roll him into the apartment and sit on the couch if the weather was bad.

I would just sit and breathe. I continued with this practice when we moved into our new house and began to make a habit of getting up in the early morning hours before the children awoke. I sit on the couch and I just breathe.

If I don't get up before the kids, I will look for another opportunity in the day to sit and breathe for five minutes.

Have you had any unusual experiences during meditation?

After I'd been meditating for a year or so "religiously" (every day), and while I was reading *The Autobiography of a Yogi* by Paramhansa Yogananda, I had a very profound personal experience where I felt a presence in the room with me as I meditated. I cannot explain it other than to say that it felt real. Though I could not prove it was there, or point to any evidence of its existence, I felt the presence of another being in that room as clearly as I felt the presence of my own body.

This presence stayed with me—strongly—for a full week. After that week, it went away, but soon after that another "outside of me" thought came into my consciousness while I was meditating: to go to the computer and type in the word "Michael." I did so, and onto the screen came a dozen or more images of Archangel Michael. At that moment a voice over my right shoulder said, "Leta, this is Archangel Michael and I have come to work with you."

I did exclusive work with Archangel Michael for some time and then, while driving home one day from a meeting with a friend, I heard, "Leta, this is Gabriel and you are also working with me now."

I cannot explain these experiences rationally. They are not rational. Yet to me, they are as real as the experiences of giving birth to my children. They opened up a new path of expansion for me.

Since then I've had other experiences that are not rational, either, but are also real. One night, for example, I was awoken in the middle of the night by my husband, who was looking towards the ceiling of our bedroom and saying, "What the hell!" When I looked up, I saw a geometric figure of light that was directly on top of us. It had patterns and intricacy that was beyond a moon shadow. He got up and went to the bathroom, and the light went across the ceiling and out the window. I said, "I saw it too," but we never spoke of it again. This was the beginning of another "opening" to other dimensions and ways of communicating with non-physical realities.

Another experience: Once, I was in the car and out of the corner of my eye I glimpsed a child. I thought it was one of my children hiding in the backseat and I called out to them.

However, when I looked behind me, nothing was there except the invisible presence of something.

"Okay. Who is here with me?" I asked.

The answer came in the form of a light being I can only reference as an elf. It sounds crazy. However, to me, it was as real as if I'd gone to Middle Earth and met the Elfin Kingdom itself! I sat there in the car and had a conversation with this elf who was telling me that I was now open to receiving messages from the elemental light beings who reside on this planet in non-physical form.

I have conversations with trees that are real. They talk to me and tell me what is up with my life from the perspective of a tree, which is a very long perspective considering how long trees live. I have also been visited by the trees in meditation and taken on journeys that expand lifetimes.

Have you ever been healed, bodily or otherwise, during meditation?

Through meditation, I have been able to receive the lessons my body parts want to teach me. I also have been expanded so dramatically that I can now communicate with angels and light beings throughout the cosmos and consciously extend my energy out in all directions and to every corner of the Universe.

Due to meditation, my inner world is just as exciting as the outer experiences of my manifested reality in form. I cannot say that everyone will have my experiences if they meditate, but I can say that what you are opened up to through meditation is so interesting, so mind-blowing and so much fun that it becomes your joy to be with yourself.

How many people can say they are truly in love with who they are? I am. I believe that the greatest healing this planet can experience is the healing of Self-Love. I love myself more than I ever thought possible. I also love what is. And that, in itself, is a great healing for the planet.

What are your spiritual beliefs? Are they grouped together as a recognized belief system of any kind?

Put simply, All That Is is spiritual.

I believe in the sacredness of the dirty diapers and the dirty laundry as well as that of the holy ceremony. I believe that if anything, the dirty laundry is more sacred than the holy ceremony because there is no pretention in it; it just is. Laundry is laundry. How you perceive the task of doing the laundry is either awakened to its beauty, its enlightened nature, its perfection, or not.

There is no established belief system or religion to which I subscribe. I am not Christian. I am not Buddhist. I am not Hindu or Muslim. I am the one who believes in the sacredness of dirty diapers and dirty laundry. I am the one who believes in heaven right here, right now, from the inside out. I am the one who works diligently to remove all beliefs so I am left with nothing—the great nothingness of my being. I am the one who examines my beliefs, my stories, and removes them one by one until I am left with only what is.

I am not here for people. I am not here to be anything to anyone. I am not here for my kids. They come for me, so I may learn from them, but I am not here for them. I nurture them to adulthood, but they don't rely on me for anything, cosmically speaking.

I am here only for the earth. I am here to raise her vibration, to bring her peace, to place her at a higher vibration in the galaxy and beyond. I am here to be a peacemaker for the earth. If that helps humankind as well, it is a blessed byproduct. First and foremost, I bring peace to my Self so the earth may be more peaceful and thus raise its own vibration, one human loving him or her Self at a time.

What's the best thing about meditation for you?

I have enjoyed making meditation and contemplation the way I am in the world. I exist with my family and do all the usual mom things, but at the same time I'm never more than a breath away from a wonderful lightning bolt, an "ah-ha" moment where I suddenly understand something about humanity or the people around me or the universe in a way that was mysterious a moment before. It is fun!

We all talk about meditation as if it's a similar experience for all. And we now know that the same regions of our brain are activated no matter which practice we use. What do you think: how close is what one person calls being "in touch with God" to the feeling experience another has of mere "rest and relaxation"?

Being in touch with God is being aware of the active, vital force within the Self—the electricity charge that animates the Self. It's what is "behind" the manifested personality and the persona you call "you" in a conventional setting. I am alternatively relaxed, rested, overwhelmed, calm, angry, loving and all the other emotions of the human, life-on-earth experience, but none of them touch my trust and faith in the God that is always present in me as a living force.

For me, God is not a belief or an idea or a concept. It is a vibrating Life Force that I feel *real*-ly, as a real experience. It is like the Chi of Taoism. That is the only way I know how to come close to describing it. Images of God from my childhood of the man in a robe with a big white beard are nothing next to this force, which is faceless, formless, timeless and infinitely expansive. It is like I have electricity running through me all the time and it makes me feel very much a part of the cosmos—no matter what may be going on in the world around me (think: laundry, dirty dishes and chaos!).

What about when you're depressed or angry or a bad mood? Does meditation still help you feel better? How often does it help you get out of your rut? How often does it fail to do so?

I rarely feel that I am in a bad mood these days, but that does happen sometimes. Then, meditation does make me feel better. I notice the bad mood and am grateful for the feeling of being in a bad mood. I remind myself that it is only the biggest and best blessing a person could ever have! Through all of these different feelings and emotions, I am given the opportunity to love God more, to experience the life force that is within me even more broadly and to expand into new understandings I didn't have before. I am grateful for all of it. There is always another night's sleep to come my way and a fresh start in the morning. I always have the opportunity to see myself from a deeper perspective and observe what is going on as I am angry, grumpy or whatever. I can notice at any moment how I am feeling and honor that immediately. When I am frustrated, I am lucky to have that emotion! All of it is a great blessing and I am grateful to be alive.

How often does meditation feel good in the moment? How often are you itching to get out of the chair?

Meditation feels good all of the time, as does contemplation. Contemplation is a way of pondering through your day seeking greater understanding of all things around you. It is a way of going through life with a sense of humility so you are always ready to learn and expand. Humility is a great force because it gives you the space to learn and grow. What you discover is beyond explanation. It is bliss, pure and simple.

What makes you continue to meditate?

Connecting to God, this life force I have described above, keeps me meditating and contemplating every day. I love how I feel inside. I love that in a moment I can go from "AAAAAHHHH!" (think: four boys all complaining about something at the same time, a house that was clean two minutes ago and is now a disaster, a dog that is barking, a husband who is not feeling well and a thousand other things that could be considered "my day") to "I love you God. I'm so grateful. Thank you."

Gratitude is always just a breath away. That is a really great feeling. I am beautifully blessed. There isn't a lot else to it. It is incredibly difficult to describe. I don't know if I have done it very well. I experience all the things that all humans experience, but I have a relationship with the inner divinity of Life (I call it God) that is hard to describe, but incredibly rewarding and incomprehensibly blissful.

Is there anything else you would like to communicate to the reader of this book?

I would want anyone reading the book to know that humility and surrender are great and powerful forces. They allow us to be moved in life to new vistas that are more glorious than anything we could have imagined. They allow life to work its magic on us. They create space for joy in IS-ness. They make the things we don't like seem like gifts (and gifts they are). They give us room to unwrap the gift and see it for the beautiful thing it is. They keep us on our toes, looking for new understandings, broadened perspectives and inner growth. They enable us to go from, "I don't understand this!" to "Oh, yeah, I totally get that" in about a millisecond (once we are practiced at it). I count humility and surrender as my very best friends in the non-physical realms. They make me laugh, cry good tears when I need them and have fun in life. So. Much. Fun!

I'll give you an example. After I read over this interview to give my final approval before publication, I realized that I sound like a crazy person! I'd put myself in a hospital for deranged people if I weren't so functioning and normal in every other way! Even though the things I wrote are true for my experience, I feel very exposed in the re-reading of them.

So, I come back to surrender. I come back to knowing that these feelings of vulnerability are perfect. It is a perfectly normal thing to feel outside of one's comfort zone as you go into new places in your inner journey. These feelings are okay. I am allowing this book to be whatever it is meant to be, whatever will serve the highest good, despite some complicated emotions about it and my feeling of lack of control. This is surrender. This is humility.

MAY
NOTICING

SO, I'm crazy again. Tolle calls this state of mind "insane," but I'll settle for the less dramatic term. My mind is a house of horrors, in which any escape leads only to an even more monstrous thought.

She's annoying. He doesn't love me. I think I've gained weight. No matter how hard I work, nothing gets done.

I'm depressed. I'm exhausted. This is hard. It's getting worse.

I really wish I could just give up.

Daily sitting meditation has never been easy for me to pull off, but in this rocky mental soil it's been especially hard. Nothing's growing. Nothing's getting fed. Often, after my five minutes on the floor, I feel worse than when I started. Often, I skip it altogether. But can you blame me for not wanting to sit quietly with myself, when myself is such unpleasant company?

Last week, in an attempt to undermine this condition, I watched another Esther Hicks video. One of Abraham's analogies hit the spot. When your car is low on gas, he said, you don't drive to the station, then sit in front of the pump discussing the problem. No—you just fill up and go. So why is it, then, that when a spiritual person is feeling anxious, angry or depressed, they turn first to analysis? They talk about the problem at great length, worry and obsess, barely glancing at the pump that's right next to them. Prayer, meditation, gratitude, surrender—these are our resources, and they work. Fill up already, and move on.

That's me, I thought as I listened to the story. *That is exactly what I do.*

I imagined my conversation.

"The tank is empty, and I need to know why," I tell my husband, who's sitting next to me in the car. "Can you give me the mileage book so I can look it over and we can figure out what happened?"

"Mollie, you're being silly," David tells me with a groan. "Is this really worth the half hour it takes? Plus the time to log all your trips?"

"Of course it's worth it. You know it is. We save a lot of money this way."

"We have extra money. What we don't have is time. Don't freak out; I'm going to fill up now."

David gets out of the car, and opens the tank lid, then puts his card in the machine. The gas flows into the car and I turn around in my passenger's seat, watching the numbers quickly climb. When I hear the click, I scribble something in my book, then get out my calculator.

David gets back in the car, and rolls his eyes at me, then turns the key and starts the engine.

———

Detachment is a word spiritual people often use, and in a way, I understand why. Only when we allow life to be as it is, without craving, can we be truly at peace. It's not just Abraham that warns us against knee-jerk problem-solving mode; many other teachers say the same. And yet, there is something about this idea I can't quite grasp: Are we allowed to at least try to fix what's wrong? Is it okay to have goals, to work towards things? If not, how will we improve?

At another Buddhist meditation session I attended during my search, I attempted to reconcile this conundrum. On the heels of a three week-long bout of depression, I went with one intention: to clear my head of a thick layer of bilge similar to what I'm trudging through now.

As I entered the small upstairs yoga studio where it was held, four open, friendly faces welcomed me, including the leader. With a twinkling smile the bubbly, heavyset woman—an obvious extrovert—motioned to the place the mats were kept. I chose a blue one and carried it to a spot against the wall, and later, I was glad to have the rest for my back; the class went on for over two hours.

The first half of the session was difficult, dreary, disappointing: meditation wasn't working its magic. Halfway in, I wished I was anywhere but there. Three-fourth gone, and I wanted to cry.

Unfortunately, I could not cry.

Having given up all hope of sensing the Divine that day, I resorted to my back-up plan: prayer.

"Help me, God. Help me, God." I thought over and over. "It's hard being human today, and I'm desperate."

The argument is made that God speaks to us constantly in a myriad of ways, and in the hour that followed, my experience supported it. After the meditation part of the class came to a close, discussion time began. First, the leader read a passage from a Buddhist text. Then she shared a story to go along with it. That week, she said, her car had broken down, causing all manner of inconvenience.

"The car is in the shop, and I can't afford the bill. I've already called in most of my favors. Now I'm taking the bus, and my internal reaction is very negative and bleak; it feels like everything's falling apart.

"And so, I do what we're taught to do in times like this: Rather than judge my reactions, I notice.

"I take note of my feelings, my anxious thoughts, one by one. And it helps. It helped me today. I started out this morning upset and frustrated, but after meditating I feel a bit better."

As the woman ended her story, I raised my eyebrows, widened my eyes, allowing her to see my surprised reaction.

"Mollie?" she said. "There's a thought, isn't there? Would you like to share it with us?"

"Yes," I said. "So you just notice what you're feeling? You don't think of a more positive thought to counteract it?"

"No," she replied. "I just notice. That is what we learn in Buddhism."

"So what if you're depressed, and you need to knock yourself out of it? Is noticing and meditation enough?"

"Maybe," she said. "Maybe not, I don't know. But for me, it is at least my first step."

I nodded, understanding coming over me slowly like a cloud. "Notice. Just notice. Distance yourself first. Then, and only then, take action?" I felt like a grade school student, a child.

"Or not," she replied gently.

"Okay."

Notice. Notice. The word dug into me like a fishhook, catching a little bit of my flesh. *I can do that. I can notice.*

And so, for the rest of the class, and the rest of the evening, I gave myself permission to feel. I didn't fight my dark mood, didn't "resist," as they say, tried not to judge myself and make it worse.

It was not an easy process.

Ever since learning how to choose a more positive thought back in college, when my depression was at its worst, I have relied on the power of the mind. Teachers of the law of attraction often recommend the same, warning against focusing on what you don't want. That evening, however, my usual strategies weren't working, so I decided to try this other strange method. I allowed myself my turbulence, my negativity, my worst. I noticed and noticed some more.

By the time I went to sleep that night, a bit of peace had crept in. But the next day, I was back to my old ways.

Noticing, nonjudgment—it's difficult, it turns out. Much, much harder than it sounds. Depression: bad. Broken cars: bad. The inability to meditate properly: terrible.

How do I give up the urge to fix what's wrong? What will happen if I do? What won't? How long of just noticing is long enough before I get to start thinking and solving?

I did not answer the questions that week. I have still not answered them.

———

There is at least some good news this month. Two weeks ago, as part of my aforedescribed plan, I read an inspiring book. Called *Zero Limits: The Secret Hawaiian System for Wealth, Health, Peace and More*, the book recounts Joe Vitale's encounters with eccentric healer Hew Len. Len co-authors the book, which discusses a healing modality he created based on the Hawaiian Ho'oponopono tradition.

The upshot: Len recommends saying a healing mantra every day, all day long, as follows: "I'm sorry, please forgive me, thank you, I love you." In this way, you will "clean" the energy of the people and the world around you, and create—both for yourself and for others—every kind of emotional and physical healing.

That's a pretty big promise, I thought after my second consecutive late night with the book. *But, it's worth a try. Who knows? Maybe this is The One, the spiritual practice I've been looking for that will allow me to get into the state of meditation at will.*

Maybe I've found my Warp Zone.

It had been a difficult day, and yet I was hopeful it would work. I turned off the lamp and lay down, placing my hand on my sleeping husband's bare stomach.

I'm sorry, please forgive me, thank you, I love you.

The words filled my mind, filled me.

I'm sorry, please forgive me, thank you, I love you.

They humbled me, started bringing peace.

I'm sorry, please forgive me, thank you, I love you.

And I did. I did love this man.

I'm sorry, please forgive me, thank you, I love you.

Love, love, love. And more love.

I moved closer to David's long, warm body, feeling the skin of his side against mine. I imagined love energy passing through me to him, and I imagined him feeling it just as strongly.

Then, I fell asleep.

The next morning, when I awoke, I remembered the experience, and swiftly attempted to recreate it. But my heart wasn't in it, and the peaceful feeling didn't come, so soon after starting I gave up. I picked up my son and brought him to the kitchen where we cracked a bunch of eggs into a bowl. We cooked, we ate, and I drank my coffee, but I did not meditate.

That night in bed, I lay my hand on David as before, trying to recreate the experience. It worked a bit, but it wasn't magic.

Of course, I realized. *There's nothing special about the words. The power is in the believing of them.*

JUNE
IT'S BEEN TOO LONG SINCE I'VE BEEN HIGH

SUMMERTIME ALREADY, and a familiar thought is plaguing me: It's been too long since I've been high.

My meditation practiced has tanked. I haven't been using The List.

Once again, I am failing miserably.

Here are some possible reasons for the failure:

- I'm eight months into my pregnancy, and I'm tired. When I meditate in the morning—still a hit-and-miss scenario at best—I almost always get heavy-lidded and lethargic. And later in the day, there's no time.
- It's hard. My mind wanders, and I can't catch up to it. Sometimes, I don't even want to; I'd rather let it play.
- It doesn't always work; I don't always get The Feeling.
- I'm feeling kinda alone in this whole daily meditation thing.

In Seattle, we don't get many celebrities; sightings are few and no one cares, anyway. That said, an anecdote about the real person behind the persona can be a pleasant little treat. Especially when it's something unexpected.

Which is why, when a decade or so back, my former boss mentioned that her friend once met Oprah, my ears immediately responded.

"I love Oprah," I said. "Love her, love her. I swear she got me through high school. Every day when I came home it was the only thing on, and my mother and I watched her together. Sometimes cried. It's one of my favorite memories of my mom."

"I know," said Patton, as we called our least militaristic restaurant manager. "And you know what? She's the real thing. It's not an act."

"How do you know? What did she say?"

"My friend met her at a dinner party in Sun Valley, Idaho, and since of course she's a fan she decided to introduce herself. She walked over to her, but as soon as she got there someone interrupted. Then someone else, then someone else. Oprah was in one of those awkward positions where she wanted the first woman to know she hadn't forgotten about her but not to ignore the others, either. So, you know what she did? She took her hand, and held onto it."

Patton leaned in closer, lowering her already soft voice. "She just held onto her hand."

In my life, there are few Oprahs (though I do have a few Gayles and a great Stedman). I don't have many role models, people who can help me strategize from a higher foothold.

Most of the people I know are pretty normal.

I don't want to judge them, or notice any lack—each is a great teacher for me. But when I need an example, someone to emulate, I often find myself reaching further.

Often, I reach for a book.

This month, the books I reached for were particularly supportive, and I'd be surprised if I don't always consider them friends. Co-authored by late channel Jane Roberts and the spirit entity called Seth, the so-called Seth books are truly an education. Whereas Abraham is more practical, easy to assimilate, Seth is long, dense and cerebral—best eaten with a fork and a knife. And chewed.

From my favorite of these so far, *The Magical Approach: Seth Speaks About the Art of Creative Living,* comes a particularly relevant insight.

"Consider a hypothetical goal as a target," he writes. "When properly used, the intellect imagines the target and imaginatively then attains it. If it were a physical target, the person would stand [bow and] arrow in hand, thinking only of hitting the bull's-eye, mentally concentrating upon it, making perhaps some learned gestures—proper footing or whatever—and the body's magical properties would do the rest."

In other words: The wise archer focuses on the target—not on anything (or everything) that could go wrong. Then, he takes the action that comes naturally. No monkey-mind stuff. No striving. No insanity. And yet—and here's the part most interesting to me—the mind still plays a role, has a purpose.

It's the tool he uses to imagine the target.

Last month, I wrote about noticing, then acting. This analogy fits perfectly with that. We notice what is. Then we notice what we prefer. Then, and only then, we act.

In the first part of the process we meditate, take a step back, distance ourselves from our feelings. In the second part we use the mind in a limited way, focusing on the target and only the target, like the archer. In the third step we return to the state of meditation, possibly finding our solution or the start of it there. Finally, we take appropriate action as inspired, and our minds help with that, too.

In another passage in the same book, Seth further elucidates this idea, making a distinction between our two minds. The big-m Mind, he tells us, is our spirit, our higher self, the part of us connected to the All. This Mind is ever wise and fully informed. The little-m mind, on the other hand, is the limited one, the one we usually mean when we use the term. This one has very few facts to go on, so it constantly manufactures its own.

As I read this, it hit me: All along, I've had it exactly backward. I've been using my little-m mind to plan, and my big-m Mind to imagine. But the big-m Mind isn't the imaginer; it's the planner, the one with the real information. And the little-m mind isn't the planner; it's the imaginer, the one who translates what our Mind knows into concrete, earthly experiences and ideas.

Who knew?

My takeaway: We are not meant to be completely free of mind, of thinking, unlike what I've previously believed Eckhart Tolle to say. Thinking is fine. Thinking is good. It's what you think about, how you use the mind, that matters. Maybe rather than having goals and being unduly attached to results and outcomes, as I have been for so long, I can have preferences instead. That way, I can allow my mind it's bit of work— imagining the reality I want to create—while yet realizing the ultimate outcome is out of my hands.

I want to be happy—lighthearted, carefree. I want to own a car that works. I prefer to have a strong cup of coffee, not a weak one, and a hot shower in the morning.

I imagine each of those things, the pleasure they bring. Then I remind myself that whatever happens is okay. More than okay: it's the best thing for me in that moment. The best thing for the evolution of my soul.

Notice. Meditate. Imagine. Meditate. Accept. Act, meditate. Accept.

"It's bad." Notice.

"I hate it." Notice.

"I prefer something else." Imagine.

"I accept what is, and what happens next." Accept, meditate, accept.

"What is my higher self telling me to do now, if anything?" Act, meditate.

Accept.

So, there it is. I can still use my mind. I can intend, visualize, imagine. It will be hard as ever to resist the temptation to plan in a conscious way, to trust the higher unconscious self to know what's best. But at least there's some role for little-m to play.

I love my Mind, but I like my mind, too.

————

And with that, I revisit my list of spiritual practices, revised based on insights from the past few months.

- Following my inner guidance moment by moment;
- Keeping part of my attention focused on my inner body as much as possible;
- Doing a visualization meditation (sensing the inner body, imagining my higher self, sending love energy or healing energy to myself or others);
- Doing a detached observer sitting meditation: watching my thoughts as they pass through my mind with awareness that they are not real. (This is the type Dan Harris was using when he experienced his most profound meditation ever—a "better than drugs" experience.)
- Doing a counting meditation using any mantra of choice. ("I have power. One. I have power. Two. I have power. Three ...")
- Repeating a mantra or an affirmation frequently throughout the day;
- Mentally noting everything I'm grateful for;
- Journaling;
- Reading spiritual books;
- Listening to music while focusing on love energy;

- Sending love energy to others around me as we talk or interact;
- Doing things that make me feel good, then holding on to that feeling;
- Being in the presence of spiritually-minded people and sensing their love energy;
- Praying to my angels and guides. (Lewis Carrol and Kryon, another channel-spirit duo I read recently, recommend this.)
- Doing the Buddhist thing, and just noticing.

I did cross a few items off my previous list, having tried them recently without success. Replacing every negative thought with a positive one was too tedious for me, reminding myself of the Divine too vague. Then there was forcing myself to smile, which was simply ineffective.

My list is too long already; I'm not paying rent for stuff that doesn't want to work.

———

INTERVIEW #3: The Intellectual

Anthony Amrhein *never intended to become a walking resume; he once told his mother he had no goal in life (something she had a hard time accepting). But when you're someone who loves to learn for learning's sake, it's hard not to accomplish a few things along the way.*

And so, Amrhein became a trained New Thought minister, then served at the Center for Spiritual Living and the Beloved Community of Spiritual Peace Makers. He earned a degree in psychology and gained thirty years' experience in the field of substance abuse counseling. Finally, he studied under enlightened master Gesshin Myoko, Master of Sound Yogi Russill Paul, Vipassana master S.N. Goenka, and Zen master Dae Gak, traveling often throughout the United States, India, Taiwan, Malaysia, and Costa Rica on his quest to experience the truth.

What are your spiritual beliefs? Are they grouped together as a recognized belief system of any kind?

No. I do not have a belief system. I relate most closely with the "crazy wisdom" of Zen. I call my meditation practice "the un-meditation". For me, true religion is like a cheesecake. And the various religions are like the toppings on the cake. But no matter what the topping, when you bite down into the center of it, it tastes like cheesecake.

How long have you been practicing meditation?

I learned zazen from Gesshin Myoko in 1977 or 1978 and, over the following three years, practiced daily for weeks at a time. I would falter for weeks at a time as well until 1987. Since then I have been practicing zazen daily. I have also experimented with over 130 different types of "formal" meditation practices. Since they all produce the same result, I always return to zazen.

What made you continue to meditate after the experience in 1978?

My ego would not let me quit. At the time, I wanted to be enlightened for all the "wrong" reasons. What I got instead of that enlightenment was "nothing" other than peace and a lot of laughs.

Tell me what your definition of meditation is—just your own. (Don't cheat.)

The word "meditation" is so loaded with preconceived ideas that I rarely use it. If I had to define it, I'd say this: Meditation is nothing more than sitting still and taking a good look at how the mind operates. In silence without the distraction of body movement it becomes easier and easier to see how emotions, desires and ignorance arise. Just a glimpse into the nature of the mind reveals that the mind is a conditioned phenomenon that operates in a series repetitive loops regardless of whether your true nature is watching or not. Your true nature cannot control these thoughts nor can these thoughts control your true nature. Thus these thoughts dissolve without attention and one's life can change completely. Thoughts are chaotic but the space in which they occur is imperturbable joy and peace. That is just the way it is. Everything turns upside down. What was once interpreted as excruciating psychological pain can become quite beautiful when fully allowed to move within this space.

Describe your meditation practice. Do you focus on a thought or image, or just not think at all?

I just sit still. It's the practice of allowing what is ... whether beautiful or not, whether blissful or not.

Is there a learning process to meditation?

Not in the sense that you acquire something. My view is that it is more about letting go of the many conceptions we are addicted to rather than about acquiring some special skill. Simultaneously it is also a learning process in that we learn to trust what is and let go of any attachment to the idea that any person, place, or thing could be permanent. When the mind is still it becomes undeniably clear that our ground of being is fluid and moves. It is not something concrete or solid. I believe that is the significance of Jesus walking on the water. It was a demonstration of the fluid nature of our ground of being.

Have you ever experienced a healing through meditation--bodily or otherwise? Can you tell me about it?

Yes. I have been healed from a lot of drama. One day I decided to read the Bible. When I got to the ten commandments I realized I hadn't disobeyed them in ages, but not because I had awakened and become a saint. It was because the drama wasn't worth the momentary pleasure.

For me, it is as though the future and the present are the same. They occur simultaneously for me. This true of all things including financial prosperity. Because of this conviction, I experience the consequences of my actions in the Now.

My future is real. The only thing missing is time.

How often does meditation feel good in the moment? How often are you itching to get out of the chair?

It is very rare that I experience either feeling during meditation. For me, the whole practice is about not superimposing any value judgments upon what is.

What about when you're depressed or angry or a bad mood? Does meditation still help you feel

better? How often does it help you get out of your rut? How often does it fail to do so?

Depression, anger and bad moods are valid sensations in my book. I sense that all enlightened masters have these physical-plane experiences. The difference is in their impermanence.

When an enlightened master gets angry, it's like when a dog barks at the mailman. As soon as the mailman turns the corner the dog immediately goes back to chewing its bone without a second thought.

From my perspective, so-called negative experiences should be welcomed like old friends. We need to take very good care of these sensations like they are small children and experience them fully without resistance. Then these physical sensations dissolve all by themselves, seemingly through no effort of our own. But we have to learn to just sit with them, whatever "they" are.

We sometimes talk about meditation as if it's a similar experience for all. And we now know that the same regions of our brain are activated no matter which practice we use. What do you think: how close is what one person calls being "in touch with God" to the feeling experience another has of mere "rest and relaxation"?

Well, I think these are probably both just irrelevant delusions. I once had a very real vision of Buddha. I was very excited and could not wait to tell Gesshin Myoko. She listened very attentively and laughed quite a bit. When I was finished telling my story she looked me straight in the eye and with deep sincerity and slightly sad concern said "Don't worry. That will probably never happen again." Then she burst out laughing.

I was so upset. I thought for sure having a vision of Buddha meant I was totally enlightened.

What's the best thing about meditation for you?

This one is going to sound odd. It's the discipline. There are benefits to doing at least one "formal" good thing for oneself on a daily basis that are ineffable.

What is your ultimate life goal?

My ultimate life goal is to enjoy free time with the people I love. So I measure wealth and success in terms of free time rather than money or possessions.

What is the goal of your meditation practice?

That's an easy one. There is no goal. I call it the un-meditation. There is nothing to gain but there is something to lose. The sensation of fear, for example, has completely disappeared from my body. But that was not a goal. It was a side effect. So when I sit I have no expectation. For me, meditation is nothing more than the daily discipline of knowing I did something good for myself. Meditation is simply a process of tapping into and paying attention to "what is" and experiencing the subtlest sensation of "what is" that the human body is capable of in this particular moment. And sometimes "what is" is not particularly pleasant. But that is irrelevant. What is important is to just sit with it. In many ways meditation is more like coming home to the body after having had a long day dream about somewhere else.

Why don't more people meditate?

Without some sort of disciplined practice people cannot stand witnessing what their mind is actually thinking and doing. It is out of control. The average person finds lack of control very irritating.

Interestingly, the discipline does not have to be meditation. It could be dance, aikido, tai chi, yoga, baseball ... just about anything. However, *one has to find and practice their one thing.* After about five years everything else falls into place seemingly through no effort of their own. It takes about five weeks of sitting meditation every day for twenty minutes a day to begin to see the beginnings of profound changes in one's attitude and outlook on life.

What is the strangest experience you've ever had with the Divine or the Inexplicable?

I've had so many, all completely different yet somehow all the same. A common denominator is that at the time I was experiencing the "divine" or "inexplicable" they seemed completely ordinary. I noticed nothing special until after the experience was over. I was completely incapable of forming any sort of reflective judgment what so ever because "what is" had my undivided awareness.

An example: I was sitting on a beach in Costa Rica. Behind me was an infinity of forest. The waves were gently lapping. Suddenly the thought occurred to me "God, haven't I done everything you asked for twelve years now? Why can't you let me repeat the bliss of my very first spiritual experience?" I was counting on God's grace, but nothing happened.

Somewhat disappointed but also resigned and accepting, I stood up and began to walk. I looked down at my watch to see how many minutes of meditation I had "banked" into my spiritual war chest. (Are you hearing the subtle arrogance in all of this?) It was then I noticed my watch had stopped.

I began walking into the woods. As I did so, I found I could hear different creatures and miraculously locate them in space. Not only was my sense of hearing heightened, I saw more than the usual eight to ten shades of green. I felt I could literally see thousands of different shades of green so that the defensive camouflage of the insects and animals was no longer effective. I could easily see everything naked where it stood. But it all seemed perfectly normal. Everything was just being itself.

On that trip I was showing my aunt and uncle around Costa Rica. This heightened awareness experience lasted another three weeks. We had conversations that were typical yet somehow profoundly intimate. Everything just flowed. My uncle who is a self-made man and slightly on the crass side was overwhelmingly gentle and kind to both me and my aunt. It was as though he felt heard for the first time, if that makes any sense. Everything had a spontaneous yet purpose-filled sensation within it. Even the rocks felt alive. The trees were treeing, the waves were waving, the rocks were rocking and so on.

Then, it happened. We were headed back home. First we drove down the sandy beach road. Then we drove down the bumpy gravel road. Then we hit the pavement. Then we crossed the bay on a two and a half-hour car ferry. Then we stopped at the first light. Nothing yet. I was still in "flow-bliss." Then we came to the second light. While waiting for it, it suddenly occurred to me that I am a business owner and I had important things to do when I got home. That was my first reflective thought involving the perception of future time and immediately I felt it enter my body. It was the physical sensation of fear. Almost immediately I realized I had been in the Zen Zone for the past three weeks and was amazed. It was my first thought of the past. Suddenly I had left the eternal and was back in the tyranny of time. I was "re-burdened" with the foolish concerns of the ego.

Believe it or not, almost exactly one year later I was sitting on that same beach when my watched stopped again, and again I fell into the bliss state. As before, I did not recognize I'd been in it until it ended with the idea of "I am important."

JULY
LOVE—ANY LOVE—IS MEDITATION

LAST MONTH, I met an angel. It happened in one of the ways these things often happen, namely: I pushed him out of my body.

His name is Jack, and he is way, way cuter than a button. He has that classic newborn monkey face, with creases under his eyes and an overbite, and a tiny little chin over a second larger one. When he was born he didn't cry right away; instead, he just looked at me in confusion. I told him over and over how much I loved him, how good his life would be. Then the nurse said something wasn't right, and took him away.

I should've known; he was supposed to cry.

As the baby headed to the NICU, I delivered the placenta, David and Xavier waiting outside. Several hours later, I was settled in my new bed, wondering when I'd see Jack again.

"They told me they'd let me know when the tests were done, but I haven't heard anything," I told David. "I'm going to just go down there."

I got out of bed, and asked the first nurse I saw where the NICU was located. Then, I made my escape.

"Can I see Jack?" I asked the first nurse I saw, a thin, tight-lipped woman who reminded me of an old-fashioned schoolteacher.

"Are you the mother?" she asked, looking at me suspiciously. I said yes, and she led me to his room.

"He just finished up," she said as we approached his bed, where he lay quietly asleep.

I asked if I could hold him, and the nurse said I could, so I arranged myself in the chair. Then I began to nurse.

An hour later, I was still there, and the nurse had started giving me strange looks.

"Do you want to go back to your room and get some rest?" she asked, sounding annoyed.

When I said no, she resorted to ignoring me, going about her duties in a clipped manner.

Eventually, I returned to the maternity ward one building away, slept for an hour and a half, then ate breakfast and returned. By this time, the Schoolteacher had been replaced by the Grandmother, and with her my presence was welcome. She gave me advice. She brought me juice. She seemed to appreciate that I was there.

The news about the baby was reassuring, and they were right; he turned out to be perfectly fine. We did, however, spend four days in that NICU, and the experience was interesting for one reason. The room didn't change. The routine didn't change. But every ten hours, the nurses did.

After the Schoolteacher and the Grandmother, we met the Professional, the Best Friend, the Scholar and the Older Sister. Then the Technician, the Cool Aunt and the Boss. Some of them came several times. Each of them brought a different energy to the same room, the same few routine tasks.

After the first few days of this, it dawned on me: Each of them affected me in some way. Each time they changed shifts, my mood shifted, too. *Do I affect other people this much?* I wondered.

Sure, I just gave birth and I was a bit hormonal. But I think the answer is yes. People—even strangers—sense what you're thinking, whether or not you care. The way we feel about them, interact with them, matters.

I don't know when the meditative state came upon me again—how exactly I grasped the invincibility star. It may have been while I was nursing Jack or Xavier, or while I was smiling through tired eyes at my husband, or it may have been something I don't remember. But I do know the reason it happened. I was sending love energy to the people around me, caring about them. Most often the new baby, but others, too. When I realized what I was feeling, another realization came: Love—any love—is meditation.

I am still feeling the meditation. For the past five weeks, it's been my companion, little Jack's twin brother at my breast. As I determined to do earlier in the year, I'm doing everything I can to hang onto it: exercising more, taking more breaks, more naps. I'm caring for myself physically and emotionally, and it's helping my spiritual life, too.

Maybe I've finally made progress.

And so, love is meditation and meditation, love—but this isn't how we usually define it. For my reading this month, I chose books strictly about the basics of meditation, and from them gleaned an important insight.

I learned that I'm doing it right.

Andrew Newberg is a prominent researcher of the relationship between neuroscience and spirituality. In addition to his work as a physician and a professor, he's an accomplished author, with several books and courses on the subject he calls "neurotheology." Through the use of brain scans, he has viewed and quantified the effects of meditation and prayer on various parts of the brain, and interestingly, no matter which technique his subjects use, the results are somewhat similar. Catholic nuns who use a so-called centering prayer and Tibetan Buddhist meditators all show greatly reduced activity in the parietal lobe, the area of the brain responsible for the awareness of space and time, and increased activity in the amygdala and hippocampus.

When I read this, I breathed a sigh of relief. I don't have to know anything about chakras, or focus on my breath, or try to stop myself from thinking. I don't have to use the techniques other people swear work for them but have never seemed to work for me.

I can meditate however I damn well please.

Because, as it turns out, meditation is a really difficult concept to pin down. While there are many similarities in the definitions I read this month, subtle but important differences exist.

Here, a few of definitions from the books that seem to represent the majority opinion:

- "Meditation is a discipline that enables a person to become more aware of the total field of experience." —*Meditation: Exploring a Great Spiritual Practice*, Richard Chilson
- "Meditation is nothing other than a relaxation technique with various larger purposes." —Andrew Weil
- "Meditation is the art or technique of quieting the mind so that the endless chatter that normally fills our consciousness is stilled. In the quiet of the silent mind, the meditator begins to become an observer, to reach a level of detachment, and eventually, to become aware of a higher state of consciousness." —*Meditation: Achieving Inner Peace and Tranquility in Your Life*, Brian Weiss

Vague, much? I thought so. Which is why I appreciated *Meditation: How to Reduce Stress, Get Healthy, and Find Your Happiness in Just 15 Minutes a Day* by Rachel Rofe. Rather than describe a single technique in depth, as most meditation texts do, it gave a lighter, higher-level view. It even included something I've been looking for all year: a comprehensive meditation taxonomy.

Meditation practices can be divided into three primary categories, Rofe writes:

•Concentration meditation (also called structured meditation);

•Mindfulness meditation (also called unstructured meditation); and

•Transcendental meditation (something else altogether).

Concentration meditation is when you focus on one thing, gently bringing awareness back to it over and over: a sound, a visual object, an activity (like walking), a chant, a concept, a mantra, a feeling (like energy coursing through your body), an emotion (like love), a visualization, or your breath.

Mindfulness meditation is paying attention to your actions and thoughts (i.e. being in the moment). This includes body scan meditation, writing meditation, walking meditation, eating meditation, chakra meditation, Zen meditation (living in the now).

Transcendental Meditation (TM) is restful awareness, and effortless. There is no need to follow your thoughts; instead, you just let them flow while maintaining a mindset of peace and rest.

Maybe someday I'll find a meditation technique I like better than any I've tried thus far, including what I enjoy so much now. Until then, I rest assured that if Andrew Newberg scanned my brain, he'd prove that what I'm doing works. My type of meditation even has a category—energy meditation.

I'm a real meditator after all.

MEDITATION INTERVIEW #4: The Artist

For twenty years, **Evan Griffith** *and his wife have owned and operated a sizable art gallery in Palm Beach County, Florida.*

Evan is the consummate artist: deep thinking, profound, highly excitable, and just the right amount crazy. Author of two books including Burn, Baby, Burn: Spark the Creative Spirit Within, *he's also a talented writer. His blog,* Notes for Creators, *is a passionate exploration of the intersection of creativity and divinity. Here are his answers to my questions.*

How long have you been practicing meditation? What was your first experience of meditation like?

In my teens in the '70s, my very conservative yet searching Christian mom brought me to a yoga class that ended with meditation. Later in high school and college I sporadically experimented with meditation. By my senior year I became so enamored with the possibilities that I created an independent study course in Human Potential with a friend—approved by the college!—that focused heavily on exploring different types of meditation, yoga, guided imagery, affirmations, New Thought books, sleep experiments and more. It sounds normal now, but it felt daring at the time, a little less than four decades ago.

The most memorable early meditation I can recall was with a candle—simply focusing on the flickering flame. We were high so it really doesn't count. But it intrigued me enough to want to try it in a normal state of mind. Once I did so, mind-altering substances utterly lost their appeal. To me it was the difference between a sloppy beer-party tryst and falling in love. Deep, life-long, *love.*

What made you continue to meditate?

From my earliest meditation attempts in college, I took to it right away. Even while experimenting with different forms of meditation, I felt profoundly at home in the process. From then on, meditation was a part of my life—though I didn't develop an ironclad daily meditation process until many years later, after an intense spiritual experience.

What is meditation to you?

Single-pointed stillness. More specifically: An enveloping shift sparked by single-pointed attention in silent stillness. You start with you and your little mind silent and focused, and when it goes well you spring through a cosmic bliss portal.

Describe for me your meditation practice. Do you focus on a thought or image, or just not think at all?

My favorite practice is what I call "love zazen." In zazen you sit comfortably and attentively. As thoughts come, you notice them, then let them go.

My method is similar: First, you sit quietly and comfortably, engendering a feeling of love or appreciation in yourself. This becomes quite easy once you get the hang of it. If you're having difficulty with it, though, conjure up someone you adore. Or something you relish doing. Or a favorite place, a treasured memory, or an experience charged with affection. Focus on that person or experience until you feel washed in appreciation or love. Then focus on the sensation, and let go of the image that sparked it.

Next, begin to observe your thoughts. One by one, notice them, then consciously fill them with the love you're feeling. Often thoughts of things you're keenly grateful for will come up. Love and appreciate them. If a thought about some difficulty in your life arises, let your loving appreciation sensation surround it, too. Find something to appreciate about that difficulty.

Appreciate the hell out of it! As you do this, whatever rises up in your thoughts will whisper away, and you'll be left with just the loving appreciation sensation.

I swear by the moons of Jupiter that I've resolved more issues this way than by any other method. If I miss a day of this practice, I miss it in the way you miss a person; I'm actually sad about it.

Another favorite meditation of mine is a listening meditation—simply sitting comfortably erect, and listening. You become attentive to the sounds surrounding you, as well as the sounds and feelings within you. If you're out in nature you might hear a brook, birds, a dog barking, squirrels skittering along tree branches, wind picking up and dying down, blowing through and around what surrounds you. If you're in a more urban environment, you'll hear cars and people and snatches of conversation. You'll hear sirens or music or doors or creaking. I've practiced this in New York City on Ninth Avenue with jackhammers going—it still works. After a while you'll start hearing the beat of your heart and the coursing of blood through parts of your body. A little while longer and you'll swear to God that all the sounds are being orchestrated together. You begin to feel part of a great symphonic movement that is being played through all the elements of Earth.

Is there a learning process to meditation?

Yes! It's primarily learning to relax into the process. And learning that sitting in silence for five or twenty minutes— whatever your commitment—is meditation. Regardless of outcome. Many people think they're doing it wrong ... they're not. Sitting softly erect, going calm, slowing your breathing down, focusing on the method you've chosen is all it is. Even when you feel unfocused much of the time. With practice, the pauses in between mind sparks become longer, more sensuous. You begin to feel the space between your thoughts ... and it's voluptuous. Rapturous even. In time that spaciousness envelops even your thoughts. It's a loving saturation that comes to permeate the entirety of your being. Soul, mind, body, the external world ... they all meld into that loving, saturated emptiness. I use the term emptiness because that space is devoid of markers. It's a complete absence of all the things we normally associate with existence. And yet emptiness doesn't do it justice. Because it's also dense with life energy.

What might you tell a new meditator to help them through the first part of the learning process?

I would tell them to take it easy. Flubbing it is meditation!

Pick whatever method feels natural to you and go for it. Fifteen minutes of Internet research will reveal at least fifteen different methods. There's no wrong way to evolve your way through your meditation practice. Try as many methods as you need. You'll find yourself coming back to one or two favorites. That's your cue. Explore those that intrigue you most.

Have you ever experienced a healing through meditation, bodily or otherwise? Can you tell me about it?

I've experienced many healings that I associate with meditation —bodily, financially, creatively, relationally. I even credit it with helping me find my life partner.

The first time I realized meditation could be used for healing was while reading a magazine. I think it was a yoga magazine, or Oprah's magazine—something with a cool spiritual slant.

There was a brief article about how meditators could stop headaches.

Immediately, I sat up a little straighter.

I'm a meditator! I thought. *Why can't I do this?*

I decided to try their simple process: After my first inkling that a headache was coming on, I stopped everything and got into a meditative space. After going deeply into my meditation, I brought my conscious awareness into, rather than away from, the point of pain. Then I visualized conduits and pipes running through the area of pain with pressure building up in them. Then I imagined myself turning a valve to off gas the pressure, releasing the tension, releasing the pain.

The very first time I tried this, it worked! Maybe only a month or two into experimenting with this game I never had a headache again.

Techniques like these are counterintuitive. We're always shrinking from pain. We unconsciously tighten up around the pain points, in an attempt to block them. But meditators— people with sufficient practice accessing that deep state of consciousness where reality plays out fluidly within the body-mind—can transform the pain with their focus.

Incidentally, I've described this process to a number of people over the years. I've never seen it work for a non-meditator.

Regarding other types of bodily healing, years ago I settled into a simple pattern whenever I would feel some kind of distress coming on: At the earliest opportunity I would drop into meditation and bathe the area with love and healing. Then that night before falling asleep, sitting in bed, I'd drop into meditation again. At the end of my usual meditation practice I would envision healing ... and then fast-forward to the morning. I'd see myself waking up and feeling wonderful—amazing—having almost forgotten that I even had an issue. Then I'd see myself remembering the issue and smiling, thinking to myself, *Oh yeah, that's gone. Love that process. I love how things work out so freaking well when I set the intention deeply.*

With this, I'd lie down and drift off to sleep.

This process has worked astoundingly well for me, to the point where I can go years without getting sick. It's only when I get cocky about it and don't go as earnestly deep in my visualization that I seem to have issues.

Sometimes we talk about meditation as if it's a similar experience for all. And we now know that the same regions of our brain are activated no matter which practice we use. What do you think: how close is what one person calls being "in touch with God" to the feeling experience another has of mere "rest and relaxation"?

It's like sex. There's a commonality. But within that commonality there's a widely diverse experience, from rote to ecstatic.

Belief matters, even in meditation.

Intention and expectation frame the meditative moment intensely. Once I believed it possible, asked for it, and then went into meditation allowing for a deep spiritual connection, that's what I got. My God was it ever mind blowing. Even now, sometimes it feels as though my neural circuits are being overloaded, in the best of ways. As though my own wiring is being rewired into something better.

Do you have a particularly fond memory of a meditation experience?

Here's a funny experience that happened with my friend Gil, who was in the independent study course with me. In a book we read by channel Jane Roberts and spiritual entity Seth we read that in a rare instance someone expands too quickly in consciousness—and then bursts out of existence. It's as though their body was not equipped to handle the sudden energy surge.

This became a running joke with us. As in, "Watch out, I'm feeling the meditation vibe tonight; I might combust at any moment."

Late one night we both decided to go down to the lake and sit on a berm and meditate.

That night was windy as hell. In Florida we get these intense storms, and this was the precursor to a particularly intense one. No rain yet, just wind that was whipping limbs and trees around. We settled down to meditate, but after a short while I became uneasy—wildly uneasy. It just felt off, eerie. We were in the pitch dark, side by side just a couple of feet from each other. The wind had picked up even more. I wasn't gripped with fear as much as foreboding, as though something terrible was about to happen.

I opened my eyes and glanced at Gil. I could only see his silhouette, but he seemed to be deep into his meditation. Not wanting to disturb him, I silently got up and headed back. My girlfriend was in my dorm room and I spilled out how relieved I was that she'd shown up—I was that unsettled.

Maybe five or ten minutes later, Gil comes bursting into my room, flinging the door open so violently he almost destroyed it.

"Whoa, Gil, what's wrong?" we both blurted out. As soon as Gil could regain his breath, he huffed out: "Jesus, I thought you had combusted!"

How often does meditation feel good in the moment? How often are you itching to get out of the chair?

It always feels good to me. I drop very quickly into the meditative moment. I almost never find myself itching to stop soon—but I would certainly allow myself to do so if I were having difficulty.

I don't set a timer or have any kind of prompt that ends a meditation session. I simply stop when it feels right. Consequently, a meditation can be just a few minutes to twenty, thirty or even forty minutes long. Most of my night meditations probably last twelve to twenty minutes.

During the day I am apt to drop into very short visualization-type meditations to suggestively pre-cast how I'd like an impending experience to turn out (a meeting, a negotiation, a conversation, an activity) or to ask for guidance or a solution to an issue. Sometimes I may be getting away from meditation and more into asking. I guess you could call it prayer. But I see it all as part of a continuum so I rarely make those kinds of distinctions in my own mind.

What about when you're depressed or angry or in a bad mood? Does meditation still help you feel better? How often does it help you get out of your rut? How often does it fail to do so?

Some form of meditative or contemplative or envisioning moment is my go-to method for any and all stresses. As well as all joys and triumphs and satisfactions. There's nothing in my life that I don't take into my practice of silence. It is that helpful.

The more I bring with me into the silence, the easier life unfolds. It's that simple.

It is so effective a process for the turbulence that comes my way, that I know almost no other way to deal with issues. I say this with great respect for the importance of exercise, sleep, nutrition, expression and loving relationships as other pillars of a well-lived life.

I'm powerfully drawn to writing meditations as well. In fact, many days a week I write a Vision Page in the mornings. I also practice moving meditation, most commonly through walking. While driving I often speak affirmations aloud.

What's the best thing about meditation for you?

That it is so interwoven with the "rest of" my life that I can take it with me wherever I go.

What are your spiritual beliefs? Are they grouped together as a recognized belief system of any kind?

I draw from many sources, Eastern and Western, contemporary and traditional. Though my beliefs align closest with New Thought spirituality, I'm open to wisdom from a wide range of paradigms. My mother and brother are traditional Christians and I love talking to them about their experiences. But I also incorporate aspects of Hinduism, Buddhism and Daoism. I am especially drawn to contemporary spiritual voices from the last one hundred years, including channeled material. The Abraham and Esther Hicks duo is a favorite in that area.

There's not an issue in my life that I don't resolve first through a meditative-spiritual frame of reference.

To try to put it succinctly, this is how I view reality:

- This realm is a playground of creation.
- It is malleable, though as with any game, there are powerful guidelines.
- We come here to hone our creation power ... and to play in whatever ways are most compelling to us.
- We choose to be here.
- We are souls within souls within souls within the Ultimate Soul.
- In the greater reality everything is permeable; we all ultimately overlap in soul consciousness.
- We live many lives, in many dimensions, going from adventure to adventure.
- Life is eternal and joy-seeking.
- We are growth-oriented beings.
- Our soul-minds mold our experiences, including the events and people that come into our lives, and it is our task to learn how best to do this.
- Love, generosity, creativity, exploration, appreciation, enthusiasm, kindness, compassion ... when we live these highest of qualities we have the greatest well-being.
- Giving is receiving (and receiving allows others to give).
- Ultimate reality is beyond my comprehension; even so, I can grow ever more in tune with the Divine Mystery at the heart of all creation.

AUGUST
WADING AND SPLASHING

EVEN BEFORE I saw the sign, I knew it was the right place—an obvious mosque, with several prominent gold-painted domes. Inside the large double doors the space was formal and lovely, with a friendly receptionist to keep everyone on schedule.

I introduced myself and inquired about the morning meditation class, then perused the tidy bookstore for a while. I was ready for my next meditation adventure, and I was early.

Ten minutes passed, then fifteen. Xavier waited patiently on my chest. After taking a brochure for a local co-op garden, we found an immaculate bathroom in which to change his diaper. Then we waited on a wooden bench next to a donation box and I wondered if it was okay that he was there. Maybe it was the beauty of the building, the attention to detail all around, but I had a feeling he wouldn't quite fit in. I was right.

From the staircase, a procession: thin, smiling Caucasian women carrying yoga mats and chatting cheerfully about their mornings. After the line dwindled the receptionist nodded at me, and I took my turn on the stairs. Laughter fading behind me, I arrived at my destination, and it did not disappoint. At the height of the building was a single, large, dome-shaped room—the perfect spot for a meditation class.

After removing my shoes, I entered, admiring the classic décor. An underfed-looking woman was setting up chairs, and I chose one toward the back. As I put the baby and a few toys on the floor next to me, the woman gave me a deliberate glance. No words—just an "I see you" and a decipherable lift of her chin.

After studying his surroundings expectantly, Xavier selected a toy and began feeling it with his mouth. His eyes moved from person to person as he carefully assessed their trustworthiness. Since none of them spoke, he didn't have much to go on.

The challenge must have suited him, though, because his studious demeanor remained until after the opening piano tune. Then, with a particularly long note or two, the piece ended, and after that the only sound was the baby.

As outbursts go, these were fairly benign. Xavier put in a bit of practice time on his three favorite words, *mama, boo-boo* and *up*. He fussed a bit when asking to nurse and as I switched sides, trying to prolong his time at the breast. And of course there were those satisfied slurps. Nothing out of the ordinary, but in this place I felt supremely uncomfortable.

After the closing tune, I looked around at the others now collecting their purses and keys. The piano player stood and returned my glance with a nod.

"You know," she said, coming toward me, "This is meant to be a silent meditation class."

"Oh," I said. "Was the baby disturbing you? I'm sorry. I wasn't sure." (What I should have said was, "Hello. My name is Mollie.")

"It's just the sounds he made. The fussing and such. It can be really disruptive. We mean this to be a serious class."

"Okay," I said. "I'll keep that in mind." (What I should have said was, "I'll go to a less serious one, then.")

Another woman interrupted, smiling. "Do you know about the open meditation times?" she asked.

"No. When do those happen?"

"Get a schedule at the front desk. There's at least one every day. The baby can come with you. You may even have the whole place to yourself."

"Thank you. That is a great idea."

And just like that, embarrassment turns to excitement: *There is a place I can go.*

Several days later, I tried it out—and loved it.

As the baby enjoyed the large, hazard-free space in which to roll and roam, I relished the quiet, the near-total freedom from distraction. Sure, I could have meditated at home, or during my walks. But it was different there. It was easier. At one point I looked at the clock and realized I'd been there an hour and a half already, and had absolutely no desire to leave.

Just fifteen more minutes, I told myself, not wanting to overstay my welcome. It had been worth the thirty-minute drive.

One month and several visits later, Xavier began a new phase of his development, one that included full-on hysterics when trying to get him into a car seat, which downgraded to mere abject horror after finally being successfully buckled in. It was so bad I took to riding the bus—and my search for a meditation home class began again.

One month later and two miles from my home, I found it.

It was one of those rooms that is so much wider than it is long that you feel like there is no front or back, just two sides: the right and the left. And it was stark, too—old white paint, a white tile floor, bare except the three rows of cheap fold-up chairs. When I first saw it I didn't think I could meditate there. I was wrong.

When the volunteer facilitator arrived, what I noticed first was her smile. She introduced herself and asked us to do the same. The room was nearly full, most participants non-white. More significant, though, was the age spread. These weren't just yoga moms like the other places I'd been. There were old people— old in the beautiful way, with plump figures and genuine, expressive faces. To my relief, there were even kids.

When it was my turn to introduce myself, Xavier got the hoped-for reaction: a cheerful welcome. I asked if it was okay that he'd come with me, and Ellie told me she couldn't be more pleased. Sahaja meditation—the type practiced there—is meant to be a family and community experience.

After a brief introduction to the practice, Ellie led us through a collection of steps. We focused on each chakra, one by one, working from our pelvic area to our head. As we waved our hands around in the air and focused our attention here and there, Ellie caught my eye. She motioned to the baby, asking wordlessly if she could hold him. I nodded eagerly, and handed him over.

Then I dove into the meditation water—and that water was fine. It was serene. It was otherworldly, even a bit distorted, like snorkeling in a warm, clear sea. Thoughts passed in front of me one by one, like tropical fish, then skittered quickly away. What I was left with was the empty water that encased my whole body, holding me up and allowing me to float.

After several minutes, I opened my eyes momentarily. Visual noise hit me in much the same way that regular noise hits when you pop your head out of the water. I glanced at Xavi, who was staring contentedly at Ellie's smile and the shapes she was making with her hands. Then I closed my eyes, and ducked my head under once again. A little while later I began to cry.

The tears were unexpected. Hadn't I had a lovely day with Xavier, running errands and taking a walk? Didn't I have a wonderful life, really? But the kindness in that room cracked me open. I cried because the class gave me the time to look within—to feel the stuff underneath the surface. I cried because of motherhood, and frustration, and joy. And I cried because I was exhausted.

When it was over, I felt no less exhausted. But I felt very grateful, too.

I still feel grateful for that humble place, and the people I've met there since. For a year or so I joined them on those plastic chairs once a week, until Xavier became too much to handle.

My meditation practice has never been as good.

Of course, "good" is a value judgment, and a highly subjective one at that. But gone are the days when I set aside an hour at a time for quiet; even five minutes can be quite the effort. Many days this month, I've skipped my sitting time altogether. Other days I sit, then get distracted.

Which is why this month, I have a new system.

I call it the meditative state tracker. It's the list I'm now keeping regarding my New Years' resolution. I write down whether or not I complete my five minutes sitting meditation that day, and approximately how many minutes or hours I spend in active meditation after that.

Yes, it's corny. But it also may work.

Here are my results so far.

Meditative State Daily Tracker:

August 1: 5 minutes sitting; 30 minutes active

August 2: 0 minutes sitting; 60 minutes active

August 3: 5 minutes sitting; 0 minutes active

August 4: 5 minutes sitting; 120 minutes active

August 5: 5 minutes sitting; 5 minutes active

August 6: 0 minutes sitting; 30 minutes active

August 7: 5 minutes sitting; 30 minutes active

August 8: 0 minutes sitting; 30 minutes active

August 9: 5 minutes sitting; 5 minutes active

August 10: 5 minutes sitting; 120 minutes active

August 11: 0 minutes sitting; 60 minutes active

August 12: 5 minutes sitting; 30 minutes active

August 13: 5 minutes sitting; 0 minutes active

August 14: 5 minutes sitting; 60 minutes active

August 15: 0 minutes sitting; 30 minutes active

August 16: 0 minutes sitting; 30 minutes active

August 17: 5 minutes sitting; 5 minutes active

August 18: 5 minutes sitting; 5 minutes active

August 19: 5 minutes sitting; 30 minutes active

August 20: 0 minutes sitting; 5 minutes active

August 21: 0 minutes sitting; 0 minutes active

Clearly, I'm not diving as deeply into my practice as I once did; I'm just sort of splashing and wading. But it's fun, and I like it— it doesn't feel as burdensome as it did at the beginning of the year. Maybe I've learned something after all.

When I made my New Year's resolution this year to remain in the state of meditation "as much as possible," I wasn't sure what that meant. Looking back, I think that part of me expected to have one full day in a meditative place, then three days out, then one day in and so on. And so far, when journaling each month, that's what I've seen: a good few days here, or maybe a good week, followed by several more difficult ones. But I see now that this thinking is too black-and-white, and may lead to frustration.

If I meditated for thirty minutes, or five minutes, outside my sitting time, shouldn't I consider that success?

And it is with this admittedly optimistic mood that I revisit my list of questions from the beginning of the year. Though it's only August, I believe I've found most of the answers already.

- **Will I be able to keep my resolution to meditate five minutes per day?** No. But I'm still working on it, still on board with the whole thing. I think that says a lot.
- **Will this resolution be easy to keep or will it be surprisingly hard?** It is decidedly hard. While the meditation is enjoyable and helpful, and, much like exercise, well worth the effort afterwards, there is often a nagging thought in the back of my mind that I'd rather be getting something done.
- **Will I figure out how to get into a state of meditation at will? If so, how?** Not yet, unfortunately. But I'm holding out hope.
- **Will I ever learn how to not be neurotic?** Again, certainly not yet, and I don't see it happening by the end of the year. My thoughts are now as always a very challenging aspect of my life, the thing that I struggle with the most.

———

MEDITATION INTERVIEW #4: The Everyman

Robert von Tobel is just one of those people. Gentle, warm and wise, he is the grandfather I wish to have in some future life.

Bob leads a weekly meditation session at his Universalist Unitarian church and has been meditating for over eight years.

Describe your meditation practice. Do you focus on a thought or image, or just not think at all?

I may focus on my breathing, my bodily sensations, sounds I am hearing, or anything else as long as it is real (not a thought or emotion) and a "here and now" phenomenon.

What might you tell a new meditator to help them through the first part of the learning process?

The key thing about meditation is to just do it—daily, at a specified time, and for at least ten minutes. There is no right way of doing it; just do it.

How often does meditation feel good in the moment? How often are you itching to get out of the chair?

When meditating, time ceases for me and I almost never "itch to get out of the chair."

What about when you're depressed or angry or in a bad mood? Does meditation help you feel better? How often does it help you get out of your rut? How often does it fail to do so?

When my feelings are so strong that they prevent me from meditating I still seem to benefit from trying to get into the real here and now. I can't exactly define how that works or even how often it does so.

What are the best things about meditation for you?

That it helps me get to sleep, and that it enables me to bear with my life's disappointments.

What is your ultimate life goal? What is the goal of your meditation practice?

I have no ultimate life goal. At 88 years old I have belatedly realized that others do and I never have! Similarly, I have no goal for my meditation practice. In fact, I believe that mindfulness would be impossible if I did have a goal.

Are you happy?

Yes, I am happy.

SEPTEMBER
BREAKING

MEDITATIVE STATE DAILY TRACKER:

August 22: 0 minutes sitting; 30 minutes active

August 23: 0 minutes sitting; 30 minutes active

August 24: 5 minutes sitting; 10 minutes active

August 25: 5 minutes sitting; 0 minutes active

August 26: 5 minutes sitting; 5 minutes active

August 27: 0 minutes sitting; 30 minutes active

August 28: 0 minutes sitting; 5 minutes active

August 29: 0 minutes sitting; 0 minutes active

August 30: 0 minutes sitting; 0 minutes active

August 31: 0 minutes sitting; 0 minutes active

September 1: 5 minutes sitting; 0 minutes active

September 2: 5 minutes sitting; 0 minutes active

September 3: 5 minutes sitting; 0 minutes active

September 4: 5 minutes sitting; 0 minutes active

September 5: 0 minutes sitting; 0 minutes active

September 6: 0 minutes sitting; 0 minutes active

September 7: 0 minutes sitting; 0 minutes active

September 8: 5 minutes sitting; 0 minutes active

Neurotic as ever, and becoming more so from this stupid list. I don't need this.

I just need a break.

DECEMBER
SO THIS IS WHAT TOLLE REALLY MEANT, PART ONE

SO, that was that. I threw in the towel. I gave up on my New Year's resolution—and I can't quite decide how I feel about it. On one hand, it's been nice to have a break. On the other, I feel like total crap.

Why the failure? I do have two kids now, and that's always a handy excuse. But I won't use it this time, or go into all the gory details about parenting a baby and a three-year-old together. Instead, I'll just say that sometime between August and September, I started to feel overwhelmed, overstructured and overcommitted.

The sitting meditation was the first to go. I skipped a day here, three days there, then five in a row. By mid-November the activity meditation habit had dissolved, too—and I wondered if I'd gone off the rails.

At the end of *You're Getting Closer,* something similar occurred, and my conclusion then was also the book's conclusion, namely: I am never off the rails. No matter how many times I switch tracks, change my mind—even fail—the train is always moving, moving along.

In life, there are nothing but rails.

Of course, that doesn't mean I liked where I was at, what had become of my New Years' resolution; I didn't like it one bit. Which is why when, about a week ago, I got the sudden desire to do a sitting meditation again, with the desire came relief.

I was at home with Xavi and Jack, surrounded by model buildings and cars. Our Kids' Favorite Classical was on full volume in the kitchen, the package's promise to pacify seemingly upheld. (Money well spent.) As the baby reached his little hand toward Xavier, asking for a toy, I smiled at him, amazed by the ease of his communication. No words. No sounds. Just a small gesture, and he was completely understood.

Xavier gave him the toy.

Baby language—the language of eyes, and smiles, and twisting, and rolling, and hands grabbing and waving and pounding the top of the high chair—is one of the most effective communication methods I know. No artifice. No laughing, when you feel like crying. No moderating one's emotions, be it extreme pleasure or abject terror. No expectations clouding the conversation. You love. You give. You accept him exactly as he is, and he does the same for you.

And that day as I watched Xavier play with his object of desire, I realized something: There is another language as beautiful and simple as this.

It is the language of God.

How much more does the Universe understand me, my needs, my desires? I thought. *I have to use my limited physical body to sense my son, and even that, even with a baby, works okay.*

As I considered the question, I felt something familiar: a peace, a feeling of love. I wanted to reach for my kids and hug them tight, but I resisted the urge. Instead, I watched them play—Xavier with blocks, the baby with a rattle—and let the feeling turn to something else.

That something was meditation.

The Universe knows me, I repeated over and over. *It understands me. It knows what I need next. I can trust my Mind to make the real plans, and forego the mind's terrible burden.*

Then came a thought I've often meditated on since: *I'm okay. I'm okay. I'm okay.*

I sat with this for a while, watching the kids, allowing a serene smile to set into my face. *I'm going to feel this as long as I can before getting distracted. I'm going to feel it, feel it, feel it.*

Then, just a short step away from that innocent enough thought came another—a first slip on the treacherous slope of mind.

Here I go again. I'm meditating, I thought, congratulating myself. *I can do this. I can do this. I can keep doing it from now on. I can do five minutes of sitting now, then do active meditation for the rest of the day. And then the next. And the next.*

No more lame excuses. No more half measures.

I can just woman up and do it.

Just then, the baby started to cry; Xavier had stepped on his foot, and not on accident. I reached for him and brought him to my chest, then stared at his wide eyes as he nursed. And in that moment, I decided to argue with myself.

I'll tell you why I don't want to do that, Mollie. It's a simple reason, really: As much as I may enjoy meditating right now, right now is not the same as always.

When I wake up tomorrow, I may not feel inspired. I may feel tired, or grumpy, or distracted. I may forget I even made the goal, and by the time I remember, I'll have already failed.

Right now, I'm in the state of meditation—I'm feeling invincible, and loving it. Why do I always try to plan the future, when the future I plan never comes?

When I made my New Years' resolution last year, I was not the person I am now. I was just a version of myself, a momentary incarnation. Just like the baby I'm holding in my arms right now isn't the same person as the boy who will go to school in five years, or the man who will have his own family.

He'll be a new person, with new goals. And so will I.

With this realization came a decision, and it's one I'm quite proud of: When I remember to meditate, I will meditate.

I do not always remember to meditate. And I don't always want to even when I do. But the Universe knows me, and loves me, and is on my side, and it will help me stay on track. I don't need a New Year's resolution, or a dumb daily tracker. I need to just do what I can, when I can—and the more I do, the easier doing it will become.

Basically, I need to just chill.

For the past week, I've spent a good percentage of my time in the state of meditation. I've meditated while driving, while nursing, while cleaning, while reading a book. But the rest of the time, I allowed myself to make another choice, one that earlier this year I would've judged as undesirable. I reminded myself gently of all the lovely things about meditation, about how nice it is to sense the Divine.

But I didn't berate myself when I ignored the advice.

Previously I talked about disliking the phrase "being in the moment." So prescriptive. So difficult. So frustratingly hyper-spiritual. But maybe it's not such a bad term after all. Maybe what Tolle means when he talks about the Now is that we stop making all these damn goals.

Maybe he's saying we need to let go of our expectations of ourselves, our larger reasons for meditating, whether it be to achieve enlightenment or just to be a bit happier. After all, all those ideas are the very definition of neurotic. They all keep us stuck in our heads, in our minds, rather than experiencing life as it is.

There's a man in my Sahaja meditation group who, when asked how long he's been meditating, always looks at his watch.

"About five minutes now," he says with a smile.

He is a very sweet man. And he gets it. He gets Tolle, and meditation, and all this "in the moment" stuff. He knows what true meditation is. It's not about everything we should or shouldn't do, or plan to do from now on and forevermore. It's about waking up this morning, and deciding that today—just today—would be a really great day to meditate.

It's December. The year is almost over, and yet, I sense this book is not finished. There's something else waiting for me, something more, a real conclusion—one that builds on everything I've learned this year.

Until then, I have my marching orders: When I remember to meditate, I will meditate. No resolutions next month when the year turns. No more systems, no more plans, no more tracking.

I'll let myself go, and see what happens.

————

MEDITATION INTERVIEW #5: The Guru

Okay, so he doesn't consider himself a guru. But **Subhan Schenker** *is the real deal, whatever that deal is: sharer, teacher, guru, guide. The first time I met him, I fought back tears for an hour. He has a full beard and long curly hair and, at the risk of sounding effusive, deep-set eyes that are pools of insight and beauty.*

Subhan runs the Osho World of Meditation, which offers instruction in meditation techniques that incorporate physical exertion as originated by Osho, a last-century Indian mystic. He invites you to visit his center's website at worldofmeditation.com to learn about his Seattle-area classes, workshops and private therapy sessions.

Tell me about your meditation practice.

I teach and practice active meditation techniques that incorporate body movement. The reason I chose these techniques is that when I first attempted meditation many years ago, I couldn't do it; it was torture. I hated sitting still. One day in the midst of this learning process I went to a bookstore and asked the clerk what I should read about meditation. He directed me toward Osho, and as soon as I started reading it I knew his was the technique for me.

Our lifestyles aren't what the monks of the past knew. They carried water, chopped wood and worked hard all day, which helped them release their emotions, allowing their minds to become less active. Then, when it was time to be still, their bodies were ready for it. We need the same kind of emotional release in order to ready us for stillness, for what I call "the Grand Canyon of silence."

I invite you to go to our center's website, worldofmeditation.com, or to osho.com to learn more about active meditation techniques like dynamic meditation and no-mind meditation.

What about people who do have active lifestyles? Would you still recommend these practices?

I would recommend that they try them. And that they try other techniques, too, until they find what works best for them.

Truth is what works.

What is meditation?

It depends on what you mean by the word. The meditative *state* is the state of relaxation, awareness and no judgment. It is the state of not thinking. Watching the thoughts, watching the mind, is the technique you use to get to that state. You know your meditation technique is working when, for a flash here and a flash there, you arrive into the state of meditation.

There are many, many people who are trying meditation techniques that don't get them to the state of meditation. They may help them feel a bit better, but they don't separate them from mind and therefore aren't going to get them to the awareness, silence and stillness that they're looking for.

What do you tell beginning meditators about meditation?

First, I tell them that meditation is not separate from life. The technique of meditation is something you have to create time to do, but the meditative state has to be part of all the rest of your life or there isn't any substance to it.

Any other basic advice regarding meditation?

I often tell new meditators that in order to finally get what you want, you have to get enough of what you don't want. Here's what I mean: For each of us spiritual seekers there came a point at which we realized that everything we were told about the way happiness works, the way the world works, isn't true. We did everything our parents and our society told us to do, but we were still miserable and unfulfilled. When we had enough of the anxiety, the fears, the worries, the difficult dances in relating with other people—the stuff we didn't want—then our quest for true happiness began.

I often see new meditators give up very quickly. Partly this is because they don't want to experience the emotions that meditating brings up in them, and partly it's because they haven't had enough of what they don't want yet. They're not ready.

Okay. Now, let's address the proverbial elephant. Are you a guru?

No. I'm not a guru. I'm not a teacher. I'm a sharer. And who knows? Maybe even that's saying too much. The truth is I have not a clue who "I" am. Any time there's a notion of who "I" am, it usually gets shattered.

Zen masters say, "Not knowing is the most intimate." It sounds odd, but the moment you finally stop projecting your ideas of who someone is upon them, when you finally decide to not "know" them (according to the mind), is when you experience the greatest possible understanding of who they are. This is also true of oneself.

Are you special?

No.

There is nothing about your past lives, maybe, that makes you further along the path than others?

I don't play that game. Some people get involved in past lives, but I am more interested in *this* life!

I appreciate my own uniqueness and the uniqueness in every person. And I have no interest in trying to change them. I do have a mind that wants to try to change others and change the world. I was a lawyer in the past and I still have the mind to go along with that. But that mind is not me. I allow Existence to be.

Existence being your word for God?

There are many words. I like Existence. I like many others. What I know is that I've experienced moments of connectedness with something that feels so big, so vast, so beyond anything the mind can comprehend, that I just know it is real, whatever it is called. And then there are times when those moments are gone and the mind takes over again.

Do you have challenges?

Oh, yes. I love challenges. When I remember that I have support, they are wonderful.

What do you mean by support?

I mean things like meditation, relationships with people who are also on the path of discovery, and the words of spiritual teachers and mystics, and their books and recordings on spirituality. There are many more.

One of the great supports is to stop doing what you don't love to do. Not filling up your life with have-tos.

Are you enlightened?

No. Yes and no. We are all enlightened, but most of us are also still identified with the mind, which conceals the enlightenment. I am often identified with the mind, too.

How does one become enlightened?

There is no way to teach that or describe that. It is a quantum leap. After having tried everything possible for six incredibly difficult years to disassociate from his mind, Buddha came to the point where he recognized the impossibility of getting somewhere that is not the mind. He sat under the Bodhi tree and surrendered—and then it came. He entered the no-mind space. Osho describes a similar giving-up experience leading to his enlightenment.

Until that moment of true letting go, we only get very brief glimpses of enlightenment. When this happens it looks so close, but it's still very far away as long as the mind is there.

It's a quantum leap. It's illogical. You can't get there by trying, and you can't get there by not trying! What a paradox!

When someone is fully enlightened, do they feel psychological pain?

I have heard that enlightened people feel physical pain but not psychological pain. They may have some awareness that there is a mind that has pain, but it's very far removed; the mind has dropped into the basement.

Okay, now I'm really going to get into it. This book is not just about meditation. It's also, and mainly, about how to become a person who is able to maintain a state of connectedness with Source "through night and day and in and out of weeks and almost over a year," as Maurice Sendak wrote. So what I would really like to know is what to do when the mind makes a judgment and tries to nudge you—sometimes not so gently—to do something, change something, or at the very least, abhor something about yourself or your life, which then separates you from that feeling of connectedness.

In other words: How do we react to the monsters in our heads?

You don't. It's not about getting rid of anything. It's about watching, noticing what's there. Becoming aware of how the mind functions is tremendously helpful. You'll be able to experience how parts of the mind push and pull you; that there are so many judgments—about you, about everyone else, about everything! This watchfulness becomes more and more available. And the distance between "you" and the thoughts starts to grow.

Where do the monsters go?

Once this dis-identification starts happening, the thoughts aren't perceived of as monsters. They are simply the way the mind functions, and they don't have to be taken too seriously! They lose their power over you.

I can't explain it. I can't intellectualize it. You have to try it for yourself. When you have a thought you don't like, notice it, remind yourself that it's not you. I tell people to step back just one-twelfth of an inch from the mind. That doesn't seem too hard, does it?

I do that. It doesn't always work.

No, it doesn't always work. The mind is tremendously powerful. It can process an unbelievable amount of data in a mere second. It is a miracle that we have the ability to step back from it at all. The only reason we are able to is that what is behind it is indestructible. And usually, we only obtain just a flash of true silence. Maybe for ten seconds you are in silence, and those ten seconds can be life-changing.

Why is this the way it is? Why is it so hard to detach from mind, from pain? It doesn't seem fair.

Maybe awareness isn't that cheap. Maybe awareness has to be earned.

The truth is, though, it's hard because it's hard. Because this is the nature of the mind. Asking "why?" is a game of the mind, the one it plays a million times a day. Why can't I have this? Why can't I do that? Why can't I be there, feel that way?

D. H. Lawrence was a very intelligent man. One day he was walking with his nephew in the woods when his nephew asked: "Why are the leaves green?" Lawrence didn't answer right away; instead, he thought about it for a time, wanting to give an answer that was the truth. Finally, he said, "I know the answer, but you are not going to like it. The leaves are green because they're green."

Your mind is not happy with this answer. But your inner being is.

The leaves are green because they're green. Asking "why" leads to a never ending work game!

"They're green because of chlorophyll." But why does chlorophyll create GREEN? "Because of the chemical reaction in chlorophyll." "But why does this chemical reaction create GREEN and not RED?"

(Once a children learn the "why" game, they can keep adults over a barrel forever!) Ultimately the only real answer we can give is that leaves are green...because they're green...!

So what about when you really do want to change something about yourself or your life? Maybe your life is going pretty well, and you already have a lot of what you want, but you would just like to tweak something just a bit. What next?

Well, the first thing I'd say is to watch that desire. Notice your perceived need to change things. Ask yourself what this tweaking is all about. That desire is the mind, and by accepting its ideas, you're identifying yourself with it. But the truth is, you are not your mind. You are much bigger, much grander than it, and within the real you there is no idea of "lacking."

What is the point in identifying with a lacking? Don't. Don't allow there to be a split between the reality of the person you are and the ideal of the person you want to be. Because whenever you have something called the ideal, you will be in conflict with the real. And if you're in conflict with the real, you will never arrive. There will never be a time when the mind doesn't want something different, or something more. Never. So, it's better to sacrifice the ideal for the real!

Then how do we ever change anything, do anything, get anything done? If we're all perfectly content with things just as they are, won't we end up sitting around and meditating all day like you?

I don't meditate all day. I am in constant contact with people. I do counseling sessions. I write. I teach classes at the college. I lead four meditation sessions a week at our center. I do numerous weekend workshops.

You see, the mind tells us that if we stop listening to it, and stop being in conflict, we won't get anything done. But all you have to do is look at the great spiritual masters to see that isn't true. Buddha, Lao Tzu, Christ, Rumi ... They all accomplished a lot and many things change around them.

How?

When I am in acceptance of who I am, Existence does the changing!

How?

Let me slow down and look at this process you're talking about because there's obviously something I'm not getting here. So, there you are in a state of meditation, disidentified with the mind, blissed out. Then the mind comes up with another judgment—say, "My child is misbehaving, and I want him to stop." This is the moment we're really talking about—the moment that repeats itself all throughout the day. This is when you decide to either reidentify with the mind and become the one who is judging, or to not accept the judgment, and just notice it instead. But when you decide to just notice the judgment, isn't that also a decision the mind is making?

No. I don't decide. We are part of an Intelligence so vast our minds are useless compared to it. When we are in a state of meditation, it is not our minds that do the deciding, but this Intelligence within us.

But if you don't use your mind, how do you speak? How do you carry out the instruction of this Intelligence—say, to hug the child, or to correct them, or to comfort them?

For verbal and physical responses like these, you *do* use the mind and body. They are tools that allow us to be part of the physical world—to speak, to move our bodies. The key is to respond rather than to react. When you react to your child rather than responding, you're not using your mind; it's using you.

Ah, I see. So you can still speak, talk, respond to the situation without using your mind to do so? Maybe we are defining mind differently. So there is the mind that's the ego, the monster, the monkey, the neuroses, and there is the mind that's a simple, useful tool, a tool we use to translate what is going on in our larger Intelligence? And so is the body, when we hug the child rather than yelling at him?

Yes, that's right. The mind is a fabulous too...but a crappy boss!

So how does a spiritual seeker, someone who is committed to becoming disidentified with the mind, make this switch? In that moment when the child is so-called misbehaving, how does she learn how not to react as the mind would like and to instead suspend thinking, then receive and act upon Intelligence, all without using her mind? This sounds like quite the skill. How does she learn how to accept a situation she finds unpleasant, without "making it into a problem," as Eckhart Tolle says?

Meditation. Meditation that really works, really functions, allows you to, for a moment, to be completely separated from the mind. This doesn't happen overnight! So it's best to start with simpler things and situations. Practice watching the thoughts whenever you remember to do so, in simple settings that aren't triggering emotions and control issues, etc. You slowly build up the knack of watching – in your meditation, in simple situations, and then, ultimately in more "difficult" situations.

Then what?

Then, acceptance comes. And wisdom comes, the wisdom that is right for that moment.

Then what? I will ask it again: How do we end up getting what we want out of life, if we're always just listening to Intelligence and doing whatever it tells us to do?

We try to force Existence to give us what we want, but this is ridiculous, totally futile. It's like we're playing the greatest cosmic joke on ourselves: We are buddhas, capable of extraordinary things, even peace and enlightenment, and instead we're acting unconsciously. We pretend to have all kinds of self-imposed limitations, including a mind that has no clue what to do most of the time, that's creating many more problems than it's solving.

It is our nature to be a buddha. Anything else is going against the flow. To paraphrase Osho: "The miracle is not when we obtain enlightenment. The miracle is when we conceal it."

So if we want to be truly happy and free of mind, we have to let Intelligence give us what it deems best for us, no matter what that may be?

That sounds like the mind talking, not wanting to give up its control to a higher intelligence that resides within us. One we step back from the mind, it loses its control and the intelligence is THERE, waiting to be of immense service!

I tell people to ask for 100 percent of what they want, then let the Universe decide, because it will!

So would you say that the main purpose of meditation is to teach us acceptance of whatever the Universe deems best for us?

The purpose of meditation is to disidentify with the mind. Acceptance comes naturally after that.

Then what? What happens after acceptance?

Acceptance and gratitude, and peacefulness and fulfillment become real once there is the disidentification from the mind. I had an early experience of this before I became a meditator. I didn't know it at the time, but I had dropped into meditation. When I was a young man I was driving my mother's car when it slipped on some ice. In the ten seconds between starting to slide and hitting the car in front of me, I had my first experience of the meditative state. The mind understood that there was nothing it could do, no role for it to play in that moment, and it said, "I'm out of here. You're on your own." Those ten seconds felt like an hour. They were bliss. And the silence was so serene, so "palpable!"

Then I hit the car, and the mind said, "Oh, I can deal with this." And it started in again: "What is your mother going to say, how much is this going to cost," etc. It was much later that I realized that when the mind disappeared, something extraordinary emerged. And later still, it became clear that this space had something to do with an essential nature that is always there, although covered by the minds overthinking.

I see. And yes, that bliss is what I want. But should I make it a life goal of mine to obtain it? Should happiness be something I strive for? Because it seems the more you try to get happy, the more neurotic you become.

You're right! Anything you desire is a product of the mind. And it will create misery around it. Do not make happiness a goal. In fact, do not make anything a goal. All goals keep you stuck in the mind. Life will give you what you truly need.

So—and I realize that I'm really trying to pin you down here—would you say that if I practice meditation regularly, and practice living in a state of meditation and acceptance, I will certainly become happy?

I will say that if you stay with it, there is every possibility that you will have more moments of feeling loving, feeling grateful, feeling at peace. And that's assuming that you are doing a meditation that works for you. Because as I said, a lot of people are doing meditation techniques that don't really work for them.

Also, be really careful because the mind that asks that question is more interested in the goal than the process. As long as you have a goal to your meditation it will keep you locked in your mind, evaluating whether or not your meditation session was "successful." Every time the meditation happens the mind will judge it based on whether or not it has achieved that goal. The mind is very crafty. Instead, be there sincerely, without the notion of getting somewhere.

The mind doesn't want you to be happy. How many times have you experienced a moment of joy and the mind has tried to throw you out of it, using every complaint, seeing every shortcoming, predicting every future bad result it could?

The mind doesn't want you to be happy, because if you are it is no longer needed.

And how long will it take for me to get there? How much meditation would you recommend that I do?

There is no way for anyone to know that. There is no formula to it. It is a quantum leap. But after a while, you will notice that you don't take life so seriously, that you have moments of greater clarity, and that you even feel more gratitude, just for being alive. These are clues that the meditation process is working.

Is just meditating and noticing the workings of the mind enough? Is there anything else I need to do?

Watching the mind is essential. But you can also find people on this path of discovery who can share their experiences and understandings with you. They offer workshops and sessions that can be of great assistance to you in coming back to your inner, essential nature!

No mantras? I love my mantras.

If you enjoy mantras, then use them! Some mantras can help you go deeper inside. Just remember, the point of meditation is to disassociate yourself from the mind.

Just watch the mind. A thought comes, and you watch it. Nothing more. This is the only real meditation. Saying mantras may be a good and helpful practice, but it may not lead you to the state of meditation, which is awareness, relaxation and no judgment.

Now, let me ask you a question. Have you had enough of what you don't want yet?

I would have to give that some thought.

If you have to think about it, you haven't. When someone is being physically tortured, and they're asked if they've had enough yet, there is not a single instant of reflection. The answer is yes.

That is true. I am getting there.

I would hope you get there as fast as you can.

JUNE (THE FOLLOWING YEAR)
SO THIS IS WHAT TOLLE REALLY MEANT, PART TWO

THE LOBBY of my local YMCA is a great place to avoid people's eyes. The tables are small, made for one or two. The magazines are numerous and up-to-date. The devices are sacrosanct. And, of course, the coffee is terrible—more a begrudging concession to community than an actual promoter of it. And yet, even here, conversation happens, if only when you run into a previous acquaintance.

In the January following my last entry, I enjoyed one of these rare gym lobby talks. It was personal, and deep, and hopeful—and fairly lengthy, too. My friend: fellow stay-at-home mother Susan, whom I've met here and there on the parks-and-playdates circuit.

Susan is one of the cool moms. She's the acquaintance that you wish had called you back, the one you always manage to tell a bit too much to, too soon, even though you swore you wouldn't this time. Her eyes are kind, her voice direct and confidential. She's smart, and a really great listener.

Susan spoke about a recent vacation, and about maybe going back to work part-time. I spoke about my ongoing search for inner peace, and my continuing quest for a flawlessly coordinated weekly schedule. I lamented the fact that I hadn't yet mastered these important life basics, and my tone may have held a note of desperation.

During a lull in our chat, I checked the clock.

"Well, it's about that time," I said. I stood and gathered up my backpack, jacket and baby carrier, carefully layering them on the top half of my body. Then I smiled at Susan and waved goodbye.

"Good luck with everything," Susan said. "And don't be too hard on yourself. It's never going to be perfect, right?"

"Yeah, that's what they tell me," I said. "But I'm working on it, anyway."

Susan raised her eyebrows. She gave a single-syllable laugh, one of those forced, uncomfortable concessions to politeness. Instinctively, I guessed what she was thinking: *What kind of delusional person am I dealing with here? Does she really think she's gonna create the perfect life?*

Though my first response was to silently reprimand myself for being the embarrassingly passionate, overconfident person I am, I quickly switched tacks and began mentally defending my statement. I flashed Susan an exaggerated smile, then headed to the childcare room to collect my kids.

Sure, it's optimistic, I thought as I descended the stairs. *But that doesn't mean it's impossible to get everything you want in life. What's the alternative? To settle? Well, I, for one, am not going to. I'm going to keep reading books, keep asking questions, keep learning, keep growing, keep working hard, till one day it all comes together.*

I have spirituality on my side, damn it. I have whatever it is we call God. I'm going to figure out how to have it all. Good looks. A great family. A picture-perfect home. Top-notch parenting, enlightened partnership, writing excellence, career fulfillment— even that ever-elusive perfect daily schedule.

And to this end, I worked even harder. I read more Esther Hicks, and learned about the state of meditation, and got a bit better at staying in it. I made friends with the happiest person I know, Leta Hamilton, and talked to her at length about my depression. I re-read the inimitable Eckhart Tolle, and—wait! *This isn't what I expected. Last time I read* The Power of Now, *it was all about meditation. This time, somehow, the words have changed entirely. I'm finding it's about something not dissimilar, but definitely not the same.*

Holy God, I thought as I read more. This is the fourth time I've read this book. I thought I'd finally gotten it, but I hadn't.

The Power of Now isn't about learning the art of present-moment awareness and meditation. It isn't about achieving enlightenment, or achieving anything, for that matter. It isn't about changing, altering, improving, learning or discovering.

It's about accepting what is.

No wonder I've been so crazy all this time, trying every tactic I could to stay in the state of meditation, with such limited success. I'm not accepting a damn thing.

At first, upon realizing this, I blamed Abraham and the other law of attraction authors I'd read. Didn't they all focus on changing one's life circumstances, deliberately creating the reality you want? And yet, there was that non-resistance thing, too, that metaphor about not swimming against the current. Could acceptance be the way we find that place of non-resistance, which then enables us to create in a free, enjoyable, non-obsessive way?

Sitting in bed the night of the discovery, I perused a few other Tolle books on my Kindle. Might they also have changed? The answer came immediately.

It was yes. Definitely yes.

Stillness Speaks, too, was now all about acceptance. So was *Practicing the Power of Now.* There was even a lot about it in *The New Earth.*

I have been meditating for a good three years now, and I've been a spiritually-minded person my whole life. I am thirty-eight years old and have explored tons of ideas on happiness, and put a great number of them to the test. How could it have taken me this long to realize that in order to be a happy, fulfilled person, at some point, you just have to accept?

God damn it, you have to get rid of all these goals, all these plans, all these techniques, all this future-thinking. You have to lay down your weapons, your armor, your schedules, your very mind, and allow life to be as life is.

I closed my Kindle. I sat with this idea for several minutes— fifteen or twenty at most. Then I decided to try a new mantra.

"I accept. I accept. I accept."

I thought about all the things in my life I wasn't accepting. (My lifelong depression topped the list.) I repeated the mantra fifty times, a hundred. And as I did so, something lifted.

I fell asleep, feeling at peace.

The following day Leta came to my house for our Monday playgroup and sometime therapy session. It was of necessity a short meeting, and both of us blessedly chose not to fill our few minutes together with idle chatter. At one point, though, when I excused myself to change a diaper, Leta did say something that stuck with me.

"Changing a diaper." She smiled. "That is what it's all about, isn't it? God is in the poopy diapers."

Shortly after making this strange statement, Leta left, and I considered what she said. *Is this another message from the beyond about the importance of embracing what is?*

Later that day, as I nursed the baby down for his nap, I decided to send her a text.

"Question about conversation yesterday: God is in the poopy diapers ... Does this mean to practice acceptance of what is, to accept there are hardships and bad moments and not to be focused on how we feel? But how we feel creates our reality. How to reconcile this? Is it okay for me to try to improve things, make my life better, or should I just say screw it, whatever happens is fine and meant to happen and teaching me and good?"

A few hours later came Leta's wonderful response via email:

David R. Hawkins (*Power vs. Force*) talks about the perfection of the rusty old garbage can. It is old and rusty, but it is perfect as that. And I think about my life this way, too. When I have to walk the dog as I did this morning and I think to myself, "I don't want to be walking this dog," I am perfectly perfect in that sweet desire not to be doing what I am doing. It is like the rusty garbage can—rusty as well as perfect.

When I ask myself, "What do I want in life?" these answers come up: I want to be with God. I want to expand. I want to find ways to go deeper inside myself and discover new epiphanies along the way.

So what does God do? Gives me opportunities for that. When I see this, I see how the walking of the dog is an answer to that prayer. I see how my children are the Universe bringing me what I wanted in the form of spiritual supply. I see how the poopy diapers and four a.m. wake ups are exactly what I had asked for.

Perfect, perfect, perfect is the rusty garbage can, the dog that I didn't really want, the evening rush to get homework done and so much more I call "imperfect."

On my walk this morning, I had a small epiphany. It came mostly because I was desperate to pee. I realized that when I have to pee, I have to focus entirely on getting myself to a place where I can do so. At that time, all that was in my mind was, "Make it back to the car, get the dog in the car and get into the store where there's a bathroom." I was focused in that suffering. I had no other room in my mind for any other thoughts.

Suffering can be liberating. It focuses the mind. It creates the conditions where nothing else is flooding us other than that one, focused thought. I was grateful. I wasn't busy in my mind. I was truly meditating. It was a meditation of suffering. Then I realized that once I peed, I'd have all this space in my mind to be bogged down with all kinds of other thoughts like, "What are we going to have for dinner?"

I realized that suffering was my friend also. It was just as much a part of my liberation as my moments of clarity or peace. When I have an expansive perspective, I see that suffering and peace are the same. They are both focus and awareness, one in the direction of "I don't want this" and one in the direction of "I do want this." But the coin is the same: eternal being-ness.

With that, I have to go collect T. from preschool, then get home to the dog, then do my grocery shopping, then go home again. Hope I don't find poop in the house when I get back, but I might and it's going to be all be perfect no matter what.

Love. Love. Love.

Leta

Message received, Universe. I've been doing this whole spirituality thing wrong.

I read the email again, and as I did so I had my own small epiphany, one that built on my realization a few months back: Meditation isn't about making goals and schedules. And life is not about perfection. It's about doing the best you can, and—and here's the most important part—accepting whatever comes after that.

Life is not about goals, or about achieving, or doing, or creating. It's about acceptance, and surrender, and being in the flow, and loving exactly what is. Susan was right to have given me that look when I made my ridiculous claim to future flawlessness; I really have been an idiot—more than an idiot, a fool—ignoring this foundational idea. Not forgetting, but hearing and purposely ignoring. Numerous times I've read about acceptance, heard about it—even wrote about it myself.

I opened the door to it, then shut that door in its face.

In many ways, I see now, even this book is about acceptance. More specifically, about my struggle to accept. In May, I learned about the importance of just noticing. In June, I learned about the role of the mind. Finally, in December I realized that goal-making was counterproductive to true meditation, and I needed to relax all this hypervigilance.

Leta, too, discussed acceptance at length in our interview. So did Anthony, Subhan and Evan.

The night I read the email from Leta, there was another poopy diaper to deal with. Then another, then another, then another. Surely it was no accident (!) that I logged (!) my personal record that day: seven in twenty-four hours. As I changed these precious gifts from my higher self, I said the word "accept" many times. Then, an unexpected result: something lifted. I felt better, lighter, less burdened. I may have even felt happy.

For the rest of that day, I laughed more easily, and if I wasn't ebullient, I was at least mostly at peace. The kind of peace that creates a space for meditation, for the invincibility star.

Of course, I have a very long way to go with this acceptance thing; it really is brand new to me. In some ways, I feel that with this final discovery of the book, my true meditation practice has just begun.

As I said in my last entry, I didn't fulfill my goal last year, that of meditating for five minutes per day. And while I increased my ability to remain in the state of meditation, I haven't found any surefire technique for getting there when I'm having an off day. However, there's something I can say now about this that I couldn't say three months ago: if there is one technique in the whole world that meets this criteria, it would be watching the mind and accepting what is there. Doing so takes whatever is, right now, and makes it a doorway to the Divine.

Maybe that's why Tolle harps on it so much.

Joy is a big blue-sky day, a wonderful thing: birds chirping, brightness you can feel in your body. But acceptance of what is, even when you don't particularly like it, is its own kind of beauty: grey, overcast, quiet. Instead of feeling exposed by the light, excited, emotionally charged, you feel sort of protected and hidden. It is a comfortable, muted calm.

I used to think meditation was feeling the feeling of feeling good. I no longer believe this to be true.

Meditation is acceptance of what is, nothing more. With that acceptance comes the feeling.

I have been saying *no* for a long time. No is an easy word to say. Yes is hard.

———

One level of maturity happens when you learn how to change what you can change. The next level of maturity happens when you learn to accept what you cannot change right now. The third level of maturity happens when you have the wisdom to know the difference. For a long time, I have known how to change what I can change. I've been great at this part— exceptional, really. I've worked so hard, created so much of what I now enjoy about my life—my relationship with my wonderful husband, David. My enjoyable, passion-filled career. My beautiful friendships, and of course my truly amazing kids.

I know that the law of attraction works. Gratitude works. Hard work works. Affirmations, meditation, reading books on self-improvement—they all work, amazingly well.

And yet. There are poopy diapers. Everyday there are poopy diapers. And when there aren't poopy diapers anymore, there will be colds, aches, nausea, and the flu. Disappointments, and —need I say it?—death.

There will be broken cars, and mean words, and cellulite and tears. Today I even saw wrinkles on my neck.

From *Stillness Speaks*: "Is suffering really necessary? Yes and no. If you had not suffered as you have, there would be no depth to you as a human being, no humility, no compassion ... Suffering cracks open the shell of ego, and then comes a point when it has served its purpose."

And so, this is my work right now. Now as always, my ultimate life goal is to learn how to remain in a state of continuous meditation. But until now, underlying this goal was the idea that doing so would make me a happy person—someone who felt pretty good a pretty good percentage of the time. I hoped that meditation would help to reshape my brain. I also wanted to learn how to connect with God more easily and more often and in a much deeper way. What I realize now is that feeling good is incidental—the goal is not feeling good, and if it is, you probably won't.

The ultimate goal is to learn how to disidentify with the mind, and in doing so, accept what is. It's a whole different spin on the thing. It's an entirely different way of approaching spirituality.

So I end this book with this final revelation, though of course it doesn't really end anything. In Super Mario Brothers, after

Mario defeats the dragon and heroically captures the princess comes an unexpected (and hilariously fast) twist: she's been captured once again. In classic 2D graphics, we witness the kiss of gratitude. Then, immediately afterward, she's swept away.

In video games as in life, one thing holds true: you never really get to the end.

Much of the time, I don't find the acceptance I seek. Sometimes I don't even try. But when I do, something wonderful happens: sadness lifts. I feel at peace.

Yes is indeed a hard word to say. No is easy. Yes is hard.

———

MEDITATION INTERVIEW #6: The Beginner

This book probably wouldn't be complete without a description of my new meditation practice, which is in many ways a synthesis of my favorite techniques in this book. I share the following self-interview not as a prescription or even a guide, but merely as a summation, a wrapping up of this particular storyline.

What is the best thing about meditation for you?

What I love—what keeps me going—is the feeling. The feeling of peace and well-being. It happens as soon as I close my eyes—suddenly, I just know I'm okay. If I'm quiet, I can feel tingling, too, particularly in my palms and my arms.

And that's it. That is why I meditate. And to rewire my brain to become a happier, more positive person. And to connect with my inner being. And to disidentify with the mind.

I should also say that I have come to agree with Subhan that in spite of my great appreciation for it, this "feeling the feeling of feeling good" meditative state is not all that it could be. I would love to experience the moments of true disidentification with the mind that he and others describe, and the feeling of transcendence that goes with it. This, to me, would be a meditative state of a higher order—really, a taste of enlightenment.

What is the hardest thing about meditation for you?

The hardest thing by far is trusting that the time is not wasted. Also, I miss being able to meditate for longer stretches like I did when I had only one kid.

Are you good at meditation?

I suck at meditation, actually. My mind wanders a lot, and part of me still thinks I'm not doing it right. But I'm really good at controlling my anger, at forgiving and being patient. At this point in my life those things are more important to me than any so-called spiritual practice. I love my husband completely. I love my kids completely, and my other family and friends. I accept them exactly as they are. And I love myself, too. The meditation will come. It takes time.

Describe your meditation practice.

My current meditation practice starts with a prayer—the same one every day—in which I repeat a handful of simple words that to me feel highly creative, energetic, and meaningful. I acknowledge that this prayer was inspired partly by Anne Lamott's book, *Help, Thanks, Wow* as well as by Joe Vitale's *Zero Limits*.

It is this:

Angels, guides, God and all there is,

1.

Please. Please.

Help. Help.

2.

Notice. Notice.

Accept. Accept.

3.

Surrender. Surrender.

Flow. Flow.

4.

Love. Love.

Give. Give.

5.

Body. Body.

Energy. Energy.

6.

Thank you. Thank you.

Life. Life.

I repeat each of these stanzas as many times as feels good.

Stanza One is more a prayer than a meditation. In it, I ask the Universe to help me successfully handle whatever life circumstances I'm currently experiencing. It's my way of getting the stuff of life off my mind so I have a better chance of entering the meditative state.

Stanza Two is the most important. It is my acceptance prayer. With "notice" I remind myself to observe my thoughts all day, particularly the neurotic ones, thus separating myself from them a step or two. With "accept" I remember to truly and fully embrace whatever comes my way that day—that whatever is, is perfect.

Stanza Three takes acceptance a step further, reminding me to surrender my will to the will of the Universe totally. I choose to let go of the need to control, to dictate each moment, and instead to "flow" with the current of life. When appropriate, I ask for guidance from my higher self regarding various decisions and actions.

Stanzas Four, Five and Six are my payoff stanzas, the ones I look forward to after the work of the first three is done. With them, I move away from asking and reminding and towards the state of love and meditation. It is no longer necessary for me to do anything or give anything; with these words, I am simply being.

With "love" and "give" I imagine love energy moving around and through me. I send this energy to anyone nearby or in my thoughts. Similarly, "body" and "energy" remind me of the energy field of my body, which I visualize radiating from my higher self to the world. "Thank you" is a moment of pure gratitude for All That Is—even the things I don't like so much. It is a thank you for hardships, for lessons, for growth, as well as for my many blessings. Finally, I say "life," my favorite word for God, to remember the All that surrounds me every day.

After this prayer, which I usually say during exercise, I do a short sitting meditation—five to fifteen minutes, maybe more. Sometimes I simply watch my thoughts, as Subhan taught me. No judgment, no failure, no perfection, no regrets. I just sit, "seeing what my mind is up to," as Anthony once perfectly put it, noticing what comes up.

Other times, I do an energy or mantra meditation.

I love my mantras. I love my energy technique, and hey, I learned it from Eckhart Tolle, the best. But these days no matter which technique I use, I emphasize separating myself from my mind. Feeling good is no longer my goal for my fifteen minutes or so on the floor. Becoming a little better at watching my thoughts, retraining my brain to automatically understand that my mind is not me—that is my only real goal. The idea is that the more I do this, the easier it will become.

Practicing, really, is my goal. And even that, I must hold lightly.

My practice is enhanced greatly by activities like exercise, reading and friendship that help me stay mentally and physically healthy.

Why did you choose your current meditation practice?

As I wrote previously, toward the end of last year, I chose to drop all meditation goals and expectations. A few months later, however, I softened this perspective and decided to make a loose daily plan. Goals and resolutions are one thing, I decided; systems and habits are another.

The practice I eventually created appealed to me on several levels. I loved the ease of it, the ability it gave me to jump right in at any time, without an extra several moments of deliberation about what to say or pray. I loved the practice itself, which was and is something that speaks to my precise individual needs. But the nicest aspect by far is its thoroughness. As a decidedly Type A person, I really, really wanted to find a daily routine that reminded me of all of the most important ideas to live by. It's like a cheat sheet for life.

Would I say my new method is working wonders for me? No, I wouldn't. Not really. Then again, I'm not spending a ton of time every day doing it. I started this book with the idea that when it comes to spiritual practice, consistency, not perfection, should be my primary goal. Unfortunately, that just hasn't happened yet. With my new practice I feel that it's been much, much easier to be consistent. As I said before, I now have a set jumping-in point each day—a ritual, a starting point, a habit. With it, I'm able to bypass the effort of decision making, which is usually the greatest effort of all. That said, it's only been three months using it, and I have a long way to go and much to learn. I look forward to sharing more of my progress with you.

What are some of the things you wish you knew about meditation and spirituality that you don't yet know?

I want to know more about super spiritual people—what they think about, how they live, what they do. Do they care what people think of them at all? When and how do they pray? Do they ask for guidance regarding each decision, each movement? How did they learn total acceptance?

One of my other big, big questions continues to be the question of which meditation practice is truly best for me. In other words: After I say my meditative prayer, what "real" meditation technique should I use? Energy visualization? A mantra? Or would it be better to simply observe my thoughts as Subhan suggests, adding nothing?

It's a much more complex question than I once thought. With the beginner's mind I describe in this book I was happy to simply do what Tolle suggested, and what I discovered on my own: Sensing the inner body while saying a mantra and "feeling the feeling of feeling good". But is this the best possible option? If I could experience what Subhan describes that I called a taste of enlightenment, that would be worth giving up my mantras for, and the immediate gratification that comes with them.

Can I do meditation my way, and still get the results I want? Or is there something I could spend my precious time on that's better?

Final thought for the book?

Acceptance. Acceptance, acceptance. Until you truly accept another person, your love for them is conditional; sometimes you feel it, sometimes you don't. After you decide to stop fighting them, forcibly changing them, even the things you once considered flaws are welcomed. After all, these so-called imperfections are your greatest (and most convenient) opportunities to grow and to learn. Even if you later choose to move on from that person or situation, you can do so with gratitude and love.

SERENITY PRAYER, REVISED

Angels, guides, God and all there is:
Help me find within myself the serenity
To accept the things I cannot change,
The things I can change that aren't changed
    yet,
The things I can change that I think I can't
    change,
The things I knew I could change but didn't,
And the things that I can and will change later
    ...
And the wisdom to see that there is no
    difference.

AFFIRMATIONS

IN MY OPINION, the best mantras are the ones you write yourself. Just to give you some ideas, though, here are my all-time favorites.

I feel the body inside my body.

I am energy, and the energy I am is love.

This is good.

All of creation is saying *yes*.

I am grateful.

I fully surrender to divine guidance.

That is the thinker; that is not me.

This is me.

This is what it feels like to be who I really am.

This is my energy. This is my meditation. This is me.

I am of the silence.

I am presence. Everyone around me right now can feel that presence.

All good things are coming to me. The blessings in my future are unimaginable.

I am breathing in light, breathing out light.

I have power.

In my vibrational reality, I have/am …

Accept.

This is the perfect moment, in every way, because this is the moment that I'm in.

I appreciate and love this hardship, because it is making me better.

Everything flows around me, while I am still.

I'm okay.

SPECIAL SECTION
INTERVIEW WITH MATT KAHN

*RECENTLY MATT KAHN, **well-known spiritual teacher and best-selling author agreed to an interview. I know: how lucky am I? I got to ask him anything I wanted—anything at all. So of course I thought of the hardest questions possible. Enjoy.***

Mollie: Matt Kahn! This is so exciting for me. I have been wanting to interview you ever since reading Whatever Arises, Love That: A Love Revolution That Begins with You, a book that relates a few of your many strange encounters with the Divine as well as encouragement and instruction for loving and appreciating everything that comes up in our lives. The follow-up, Everything Is Here to Help You: A Loving Guide to Your Soul's Evolution, is even more detailed and practical. So, first, thank you.

A year and a half ago, during one of the most difficult experiences of my life, I attended one of your live events. My friend drove me there and parked on the street, and after getting out of the car I immediately threw up. Once inside the venue, I went to the bathroom and cleaned myself up, then sat on the floor near the door while my friend held our place in line. I wanted so badly to learn how to love this—my nausea—but there was nothing inside of me that felt any amount of love. I just had no strength left. I wanted to talk to you after the meeting to ask you what to do, but I didn't. Instead, I overheard a woman behind me telling her friend that she asked you what to do about her depression. You told her to "Be the best depressed person you can possibly be." I didn't understand this then, but I never forgot it, and I think I'm starting to understand it now. Can you tell me what you meant by this statement?

Matt: Using that example, I was pointing someone towards embracing the circumstances of depression, instead of being in opposition to it. In order for us to make peace with depression and use it as an evolutionary catalyst, it cannot be wrong to be depressed. It certainly isn't comfortable or convenient, but the moment it isn't wrong to be exactly as we are, we create space for a deeper reality to shine through. In the same way, your nausea isn't preferred, but it's here to be welcomed, honored, and respected for the role it plays in your journey. We don't have to love the experience of nausea, in order to recognize how the one who feels so helpless, tired, and disempowered is the one who needs our loving support the most. From this space, we are no longer lost in our opinions about things, so we may be the best supporters of however our experiences unfold. This is the heart of true acceptance.

Mollie: What do you tell people who simply cannot love what they're experiencing right now?

Matt: I say that we only think we cannot love because we don't feel love as an emotion. Instead of thinking of love as a feeling to conjure or capture, it begins as a willingness to support ourselves or others no matter the details in view. Love is a response of empathy; when we see how deeply other people or even ourselves tend to hurt along our healing journeys, the awakening of love is a response of greater support to those in need. The more often we support ourselves and others in moments that matter most, the more supported we feel by the Universe, which at that point, manifests the feelings of well-being that everyone yearns to feel. Love is a willingness to be the most helpful person to the parts of you that hurt the most. This is the first bold step in cultivating heart-centered consciousness.

Mollie: So really walk me through this. You're sitting there really not loving what is arising. Maybe you have chronic pain or a broken heart. Then you consciously shift your thoughts to "I love this, I accept this, This is what is meant to be, This is good." But you can't hold that thought for long, so soon your mind wanders back to thoughts of hating your circumstance. What then? I find there are only so many times I can think the thought, "This is good" before I just get bored and a little annoyed at myself for repeating this stupid

mantra, and more than a little annoyed that I am annoyed. What then? Do I try to just switch to a different subject in my mind?

Matt: The trick is not trying to love the circumstance or feeling, but embracing the one who feels exactly as they do. We love the one who judges and hates, even though we may not love the act of judging or hating. Even the one who hates to judge is only here to be loved. The confusion is when someone is trying to love their experiences, instead of embracing the one having experiences. This is the crucial distinction that transforms self-love from daunting and dogmatic into an authentic and uplifting heartfelt communion.

Mollie: Can you tell me about a time in your life when you weren't able to love what was in front of you—at least not at first—but then successfully shifted that feeling? How did you do it?

Matt: I've never tried to love what was in front of me because that would be denying the realism and honesty of my subjective human experience. Instead, I witnessed my feelings, beliefs, desires, and conclusions as parts that were waiting in line to seen through the eyes of acceptance and honored for being a unique aspect of my soul. I always knew the invitation was to love what arises within myself, while honoring any external play of circumstance as the perfect sequence of events to remind me where to send love in myself next.

Mollie: Lately, when I am not loving what I'm experiencing, I'm often able to shift my attitude quite a bit by reminding myself that this feeling or circumstance is my greatest teacher, the absolute

best way for me to learn what I need to learn on this earth. For example, when I notice sadness, I remind myself to feel the sadness, to welcome it, because it is with me for some reason that I might not understand quite yet. Is loving what arises more about loving what comes of the pain, rather than about loving the experience of the pain? Or is it preferable to try to shift the painful feeling as well?

Matt: Loving what arises is about steadfast companionship. To welcome the pain, curiosities, worries and concerns, along with each and every insight that is birthed in the aftermath of loss or change allows us to be the parent we may never have had, the partner we are waiting to encounter, or the reliable friend who is always here to remind us how deeply we matter. When we take the time to befriend our feelings, the Universe steps forward to serve the evolution of our highest potential.

Mollie: Is your life hard? Is life supposed to be hard? At least sometimes?

Matt: My life isn't hard. It's exciting, sometimes exhausting, but its simply a matter of the balance I keep throughout my life. Life is hard when we forget its a process. A process is a chain of events that only unfold in time. So if we are not at peace with time, we rarely have time for the processes that matter most, which is the evolution of our soul. As we begin living on life's terms and conditions by allowing the process of spiritual growth to be embraced throughout our day, we find deeper perspectives opening up, where a life that once seemed so difficult is now exciting at every turn. The difference between the two is how open we allow our hearts to be.

Mollie: You have mentioned something called "karmic clearing," noting that we all need to feel negative feelings at times in order to clear them from the world. Why is this? What is the theological explanation? I would love to believe this is true–that my suffering has practical value for the world–but I'm skeptical.

Matt: Any notion of individual healing could only be our individual experience of clearing outdated patterns of ancestry as our personal contribution towards healing the collective. Our experiences may seem individual in nature, but it is always our unique experience of healing the whole that reveals astonishingly global implications through our willingness to heal. Additionally, perhaps the skeptical one is only using skepticism to request more loving attention, appearing to need answers and information, when it's just an innocent way to request the gift of your attention.

Mollie: What spiritual practices do you keep up with regularly? How strict are you?

Matt: I am not strict at all. I meditate, breathe, send blessings to humanity, and love my heart on a daily basis, but only when I get the intuitive nudge to do it. I maintain a daily practice not only to continue my life-long exploration, but to practice for those who need it most, but aren't in a position to open their hearts just yet.

Mollie: Do you practice self-inquiry? If so, is this an important practice for you? Do you recommend it?

Matt: I ask very intriguing questions, but only because my exploration is how I download new teachings to offer. Self-inquiry can be very beneficial, but it has a short shelf-life. The best approach to any process, including self-inquiry is to prepare to be without it. If not, you are subconsciously asking life to continually give you things to work out through your inquiry. If you can engage inquiry from the stand point of always moving beyond it, it can offer benefit. Especially knowing, it is not the inquiry that heals you, but the amount of attention you are offering neglected and repressed parts of yourself that represent the true keys to inner freedom. Undivided attention is the grace of love in action. It is life's eternal liberator. Self-inquiry merely gives you a framework to face yourself directly.

Mollie: I've heard you mention the law of attraction and note that at some point we focus less on "moving around the furniture of our lives" —improving our outward circumstances—and more on increasing our inner joy instead. Is this true for you? At some point did you stop striving to improve the outward circumstances of your life, and focus only on internals instead, or do you still do some of both?

Matt: In each and every moment, life shows us exactly what each moment asks of us. If spending too much time waiting for things to be different, we overlook the fact that anything attracted into reality could only be a catalyst of our highest evolution. This is why I wrote, "Everything is Here to Help You". While we should always envision greater circumstances for ourselves and others, it is our willingness to ask, "how is this circumstance giving me the chance to face my most vulnerable parts and shine even brighter?" that determines the trajectory of our soul's evolution. Simply put, life only appears to not give you what you want while preparing you to have things beyond your wildest imagination. With faith in life's cosmic plan and a willingness to love ourselves throughout it all, experiences deeper than loss and gain are given permission to be.

Mollie: I'm a hard worker, a doer by nature. I love lists, plans and goals. You seem more laid-back. How do you feel about striving toward goals? Is this something you recommend we do, given that our goals are healthy and peace-promoting? Or would you rather we wing it and let the universe take us somewhere we might never have planned to go?

Matt: It's a balance of both. I have goals but I go about them from a peaceful space of being. Out of the being, the doing can be done with gentleness, precision, and ease. When we are solely focused on the outcome, we are not fulfilling each task in alignment with our soul, but attempting to outrun the hands of time to capture what we fear we were never meant to have. If it's meant to be, it will come, which requires destiny along with our participation in taking inspired deliberate action.

Mollie: Do you listen for divine guidance for your actions—say, when to go wash the car or feed the dog? What is the terminology you use for this?

Matt: My intuition is always active and flowing. For me, there is a perfect time for everything and when I get that message, I follow through without hesitation. Like stomach grumbles that remind you when to eat, my intuition guides my every move without me having to micromanage anything. It's just the joy of following the flow of each instinct. It's a visceral flow of inspiration, not a mental calculation of any kind.

Mollie: Thank you, Matt. Sincerely.

Matt: Thank you.

Dear reader,

We hope you enjoyed reading *The Power Of Acceptance*. Please take a moment to leave a review, even if it's a short one. Your opinion is important to us.

Discover more books by Mollie Player at

https://www.nextchapter.pub/authors/mollie-player

Want to know when one of our books is free or discounted? Join the newsletter at

http://eepurl.com/bqqB3H

Best regards,

Mollie Player and the Next Chapter Team

You might also like:
Fights You'll Have After Having a Baby by Mollie Player

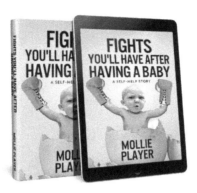

To read the first chapter for free, head to:
https://www.nextchapter.pub/books/fights-youll-have-after-having-a-baby

ALSO BY MOLLIE PLAYER

Fights You'll Have After Having a Baby: A Self-Help Story

My Byron Katie Detox: One Year of Questioning My Unhelpful Thoughts

You're Getting Closer: One Year of Finding God and a Few Good Friends

The Naked House: Five Principles for a More Peaceful Home

What I Learned from Jane

Unicorn

Being Good

ABOUT THE AUTHOR

Author and mental health counselor in training Mollie Player is just a regular person. But that doesn't mean she can't attempt feats of great strength. Like not arguing with her spouse. Homeschooling her kids. And, of course, finding inner peace. Her plans don't always work out, but when they do, the results are awesome. And when they don't, well, it keeps things interesting.

Get her free ebooks and online serials at mollieplayer.com.

The Power Of Acceptance
ISBN: 978-4-86752-185-4

Published by
Next Chapter
1-60-20 Minami-Otsuka
170-0005 Toshima-Ku, Tokyo
+818035793528

21st July 2021

Lightning Source UK Ltd.
Milton Keynes UK
UKHW010634010821
388068UK00001B/206

9 784867 521854